FOUR-FOOTED MINISTERS IN FORMATION

FOUR-FOOTED MINISTERS IN FORMATION

A Training Manual on Dog Ministry

Written by
Jerilyn E. Felton
with the assistance of
Sister Josephine Pelster, S.S.M.O.
And
Barbara Miller
Aided by the Four-Footed Ministers
Alya and Caterina

iUniverse, Inc.
Bloomington

FOUR-FOOTED MINISTERS IN FORMATION
A Training Manual on Dog Ministry

iUniverse books may be ordered through booksellers or by contacting:

iUniverse
1663 Liberty Drive
Bloomington, IN 47403
www.iuniverse.com
1-800-Authors (1-800-288-4677)

ISBN: 978-1-4759-7208-5 (sc)
ISBN: 978-1-4759-7209-2 (ebk)

Library of Congress Control Number: 2013901351

Printed in the United States of America

iUniverse rev. date: 02/19/2013

CONTENTS

To the Residents of Maryville
and my late husband,

Mr. George C. Felton

George C. Felton and Alya
Photo by Ms. Kathy K. Conrow, 2007

ACKNOWLEDGEMENTS

Since I began dog ministry as a class project in 1998, I have been constantly aware of the fact that I stand on the shoulders of those who have gone before me. I cannot adequately thank the mentors, professors, and dog trainers for their gift of loving support of our efforts to bring this present work to the ministerial community.

A special thanks goes to those who were directly involved in both the research study and the ongoing project:

Mr. Tom Miller
our photographer, who is responsible for the photos within this work
with the exception of the ones taken by
Ms. Cathy Edwards
and
Ms. Kathryn K. Conrow
whose contributions are here acknowledged;
The Sisters of the Holy Names of Jesus and Mary
a congregation of dedicated women who recognized the importance of dog ministry and
provided a generous grant to support the research study at Maryville Nursing Home;
Ms. Kathleen Parry, Administrator,
and
The Staff at Maryville
for their gracious support of this project;
Barbara Miller, and our first Four-Footed Minister, Caterina; with
Alya, the second Four-Footed Minister;
and finally
Sister Josephine Pelster, SSMO, and the Sisters of St. Mary of Oregon,
who saw this new ministerial form as a way to fulfill Maryville's mission statement
to provide
"Service with Love".

I thank you all for your contributions to this work and I look forward to collaborating with you as the Four-Footed Ministers Pastoral-Care Program continues to unfold at Maryville. Our efforts will assist residents, families, and staff as we journey to God's Kingdom where all will be welcome—both two-legged and four-legged beings.

INTRODUCTION:
SPIRITUAL INTERACTIONS WITH DOGS REVEAL A NEED FOR STRUCTURE

To paraphrase the great Lao Tzu, an academic journey of many miles began with a single question. That question was, very simply, how a lay minister might take his or her dog to work. This question on how to integrate a canine companion into ministry with elders was the driving force for research that spanned several years. While there were many ministers visiting patients with their dogs,[1] it appeared that there was no comprehensive, sustainable program in healthcare settings that provided an overarching structure for ministerial interactions integrating dogs.[2]

After many years of study, this structure for dog ministry became a reality. There was more research being conducted on the human-animal bond, and the empirical data from these studies highlighted the many benefits of these interactions. Though mentioned in literature early on as a possible benefit,[3] the 'spiritual' benefit from animal interactions had not been systematically explored.

One reason for this lack of exploration could be the fact that 'spiritual' benefits pose a particular problem for scientific research design.

> There is a contrast between much of clinical research and spiritual care research. For example, in the world of clinical research there is often consensus on scientific definitions, methods, and anticipated outcomes. By contrast, the field of spiritual care research lacks consensus about the definition of spirituality. Neither is there agreement on the anticipated therapeutic outcomes of spiritual care interventions. Measuring spiritual care interventions is difficult and their effect seems elusive.[4]

Though this might be true, those involved in spiritual/pastoral care realize that stories provide the way of dealing with the 'heart' component of the human person. Stories become the link to other human beings for those who find themselves in a nursing home due to age (loss of youth) or illness (loss of health). It is through a listening presence that care and

---

[1]   Ann Howie, "Animal-Assisted Therapy Services," *Interactions* 16, no. 2 (May 1998): 9-10.

[2]   Some of the problems to this approach will be discussed in Unit One, Lesson 1.1.

[3]   Judith Gammonley and Judy Yates, "Pet Projects: Animal-Assisted Therapy in Nursing Homes," *Journal of Gerontological Nursing* 17, no. 1 (1991): 13-14.

[4]   Mary E. Johnson, et. al, "Mayo Clinic's Approach to Promoting Spiritual Research Reviewed," *Vision* 20, no. 4 (2010): 22.

comfort are rendered in a ministerial setting; this is the place where someone is present for another listening to their story.[5]

In order to present the case for the integration of a dog into this holy work, the researcher laid down theological and theoretical grounds for dog ministry[6] in her first thesis. She continued to develop this emerging model in a second thesis that consisted of a very small research study of prayer-group, faith-sharing sessions. These prayer-service, faith-sharing sessions involved independent elders in a parish setting who interacted with a Pet Partners®-registered[7] therapy dog over the course of a five-day study. This study, discussed in Unit One, Lesson 1.2, used a structure built on the observation that dogs are social lubricators who facilitate community through their being totally present to the humans in that community. Dogs seem to possess the quality of being totally 'into' the moment. Moreover, "patients who are body conscious and feel unappealing to others, such as stroke patients, cancer patients, and patients with AIDS, can improve their self-esteem and self-acceptance by associating with animals."[8] Dog ministry as a pastoral-care tool appeared to be supported by this research study, but more work was needed.

The second qualitative research study, discussed in Unit Two, formed the basis for the formal, comprehensive, and systematic program that is outlined in Unit Four. Senior citizens who were long-term-care residents in a nursing-care facility were asked to participate in a qualitative-research study to see how dogs might make a difference in their spiritual lives. The qualitative-study participants were invited to interact with a volunteer and their Pet Partners®-registered 'Four-Footed Minister' through gently directed spiritual-care interventions. These explorations were conducted in one-on-one interactions and group-prayer gatherings. A definite structure for canine-assisted ministerial interactions for both types of interventions took shape as the study progressed. The discussion of this nine-month qualitative study includes a description of the proposal, summaries of the Maryville research study notes on the topics of general visitation as well as the selected notes on pet grief-support gatherings, and the final interview assessment. From the work so far, it appears that the CAM/PS model based on Pet Partners® protocols preliminarily provides a viable framework for the inclusion of dogs in ministry. The program developed is one that is "road-tested," safe, effective in a spiritual/pastoral-care sense, and repeatable.

---

[5]   See James M. Kouzes and Barry Z. Posner, *The Leadership Challenge*, 3rd ed. (San Francisco: Jossey-Bass, 2002), 88-89, where they discuss the areas of serious emperically based research that supports the power of stories that human beings appreciate instinctively.

[6]   Jerilyn E. Felton, "Four-Footed Ministers: A Roman Catholic Lay Pastoral Care Model for the Use of Canine Companions in Ministry to the Elderly in Retirement Communities" (Marylhurst University, 2002) and Jerilyn E. Felton, "Four-Footed Ministers: Their Theology of Presence—a Research Study on CAM/PS (Canine-Assisted Ministry/Pastoral and Spiritual Care)" (Marylhurst University, 2005).

[7]   The Four-Footed Ministers Pastoral-Care Program is built upon the CAM/PS Model that was constructed on the protocols defined by the Pet Partners® program outlined in the *Student Manual, Pet Partners® Team Training Course.*

[8]   Beth E. Barba in her article, "The Positive Influence of Animals: Animal-Assisted Therapy in Acute Care," *Clinical Nurse Specialists* 9 no.4 (1995): 200, paraphrased the work of David A. Strickland's article, "Furry Therapists Boost Staff, Too," *Medical World News* 32, no.1 (Jan 1991): 47.

This manual is specifically directed to chaplains/directors of spiritual/pastoral care in nursing-home facilities who recognize from their own experience, supported by nursing-care peer-reviewed journals, that there are many possible spiritual/pastoral-care benefits that can be realized from integrating dogs into ministry to patients/residents. The program outlined in these pages should enable these professionals to use this program as a template for their own set of protocols and other operational forms.

The Four-Footed Ministers Pastoral-Care Program discussed in Units Three, Four, and Five will provide the chaplain/director with a hands-on, self-directed guide for this "road-tested", safe, effective, and repeatable plan that has the potential for offering the highest level of spiritual/pastoral care. In addition, Unit Five specifically addresses issues of how the chaplain/director might sell the idea to administration and infection control, listing helpful hints on dealing with possible negative resistance that potential change might generate.[9] As the Four-Footed Ministers Pastoral-Care Program presents a ready-made volunteer program that is based on time-tested Pet Partners® protocols, administration and infection control should be satisfied that this program would have an impressive positive impact on the facility overall.

The appendices will provide the chaplains/directors with the templates on the components of the program. Appendix A details the research notes that formed the foundation for the discussion found in Unit Two. Appendix B consists of sample job descriptions, sample ads for recruiting volunteers that can be put into newsletters and posted to the web, a volunteer-training lesson plan, a sample of the program description for a volunteer handbook, and sample forms for use by both volunteer and spiritual/pastoral-care provider teams. Appendix C consists of samples of theological reflections and their assessments that illustrate how it is possible to find and use dog and animal stories to spark storytelling in a prayer group, leading to the discovery of how sharing personal pet stories can connect each individual to God. Appendix D provides the specific protocols that govern the running of the program within the Maryville facility that could be used as templates to formulate protocols for a healthcare facility. Finally, Appendix E contains samples of training slides and scripts that can be modified as needed, useful for training staff and volunteers. These provide a starting point for chaplains/directors of spiritual/pastoral care from which they can develop their own training presentations for use in their unique program.

In the final analysis, this work is the culmination of a journey of ministry begun many years ago. It forms a beginning for many other journeys that might be taken by chaplains/directors of spiritual/pastoral care into the realm of dog ministry. Blessings on *your* journey.

---

[9] See Unit Five where the chaplain/director will receive tips from the business world that deal with a specific outline for anticipating resistance. Further, Unit Five presents concrete suggestions on how to create enthusiasm for an in-house dog-ministry program.

Bibliography

Barba, Beth E. "The Positive Influence of Animals: Animal-Assisted Therapy in Acute Care." *Clinical Nurse Specialist* 9, no. 4 (1995): 199-202.

Felton, Jerilyn E. "Four-Footed Ministers: A Roman Catholic Lay Pastoral Care Model for the Use of Canine Companions in Ministry to the Elderly in Retirement Communities." Marylhurst University, 2002.

_____. "Four-Footed Ministers: Their Theology of Presence—a Research Study on CAM/PS (Canine-Assisted Ministry/Pastoral and Spiritual Care)." Marylhurst University, 2005.

Gammonley, Judith, and Judy Yates. "Pet Projects: Animal Assisted Therapy in Nursing Homes." *Journal of Gerontological Nursing* 17, no. 1 (1991): 12-15.

Johnson, Mary E., Dorothy Bell, Mary Eliot Crowley, and Katherine Piderman. "Mayo Clinic's Approach to Promoting Spiritual Research Reviewed." *Vision* 20, no. 4 (2010): 21-22.

Kouzes, James M., and Barry Z. Posner. *The Leadership Challenge*. San Francisco: Jossey-Bass, A Wiley Company, 2002. Reprint, 3rd.

UNIT ONE

GONE TO THE DOGS—LITERALLY

LESSON OVERVIEW:

This unit acknowledges a Florida program doing dog ministry as well as introduces the structure of the CAM/PS model (canine-assisted ministry/pastoral and spiritual care) with a brief history of the model's development.

LESSON OBJECTIVES:

- ❖ To learn about one "regional program" for dog ministry, contrasted with a comprehensive model for using dogs in ministry.
- ❖ To define the CAM/PS model with a brief summary of its history.

Lesson 1.1: A 'Local' Dog-Ministry Program

Many within the ministerial ranks have recognized the importance of the relationship of the human being to their dog and have stepped forward to share their animal with those who can no longer care for or have an animal of their own. One dog trainer has even developed a program, Canine Crusaders, which functions within her own faith community at St. Luke's United Methodist Church, Orlando, Florida. The aim of the program is to reach out to the elderly and sick, providing them with comfort and care from a faith-community member and their "four-footed minister."[1] While this local program has discovered the value of the spiritual connection,[2] there exist unforeseen challenges that have been addressed in the Four-Footed Ministers Pastoral-Care Program. This latter program was formalized and defined through a qualitative nine-month study at Maryville Nursing Home in Beaverton, Oregon. While this study was but a preliminary one and there is more work to be done, the Four-Footed Ministers Pastoral-Care Program is built upon the model for animal-assisted interventions highlighted in the Pet Partners® training program.[3] The Four-Footed Ministers Pastoral-Care Program is a solid first step in providing a comprehensive program for dog ministry that is "road-tested," safe, effective, and repeatable.

While there might exist other local programs in the US, the Canine Crusaders program is a good one for comparison because this program highlights issues that are often overlooked in program design, such as adequate documentation of the program's protocols, documentation of accidents if they should occur, and documentation of spiritual/pastoral-care interactions as needed. Moreover, since the Canine Crusaders program has not been extensively developed in a written form and depends heavily on the work of the founder, its longevity beyond the founder's involvement might be considered questionable. The Four-Footed Ministers Pastoral-Care Program has addressed these challenges.

Thus, while this local program is a step in the right direction, the Four-Footed Ministers Pastoral-Care Program provides template forms for visitation documentation, job descriptions for two specifically defined volunteer roles, application forms, a training lesson plan, and recruitment samples (see Appendix B—Program Forms). Based on Pet Partners® protocols, the ministerial protocols (see Appendix D—Maryville's Four-Footed Ministers Pastoral-Care Program Protocols) will ensure safe interactions between the volunteer, the dog, and the patient/resident. While it is difficult to determine "empirically measurable results" in pastoral care[4] and these are not immediately evident, the stories of those who minister with their dogs testify to the miracles that occur when a four-footed minister is present. Finally, a formalized program makes it possible for the continuation of the program beyond the life of

---

[1] Canine Crusaders already has a 10-year history of success. The founder, Ms. Valerie Almos, functions as the trainer for the volunteer teams through a once-a-year series of six weeks of obedience training and two weeks of on-the-job training. She has a group of volunteers who assist her in her efforts in training, testing, and helping volunteers who visit nursing homes and hospitals in the area.

[2] Gammonley and Yates, "Pet Projects," 14.

[3] Delta Society, *Pet Partners® Team Training Course Manual* (Bellevue, WA: Delta Society, 2008).

[4] Mary E. Johnson, et al, "Mayo Clinic's Approach to Promoting Spiritual Research Reviewed," *Vision* 20, no. 4 (2010): 22.

the originator as well as continued development and refinement over time as new challenges arise and are met and conquered.

Lesson 1.2: What is the CAM/PS Model?

The CAM/PS model is a structure for the interactions between a volunteer/ spiritual/ pastoral-care provider and a patient/resident where the dog acts as a social lubricator to facilitate first physical, then 'spiritual' interactions. Physical interactions that establish the caring relationship between the volunteer/spiritual/pastoral-care provider (owner) and their dog are the basis for relationships formed with other human persons. From that solid base of care, concern, and respect built over the life of this relationship, the team can more easily connect to the patient/resident who loves dogs and loves to be in their presence. It is important to note that the aim of the interaction is not only sharing the beautiful gift of the dog with the patient/resident, but also to help that person connect to God. In the CAM/PS model, the goal is the spiritual/pastoral care of the individual. Thus, by its nature, CAM/PS is neither a meet-and-greet modality nor a formal therapeutic interaction; it falls somewhere in the middle. While its focus is the well-being of the person served, the therapeutic value is to be found in the spiritual/pastoral plane where, as was previously mentioned, these therapeutic interactions are not empirically measurable in the strict sense of the word.

Structures of the Program

Based on the above interactions, the Four-Footed Ministers Pastoral-Care Program has two related structures. The first is that of a 'one-on-one' interaction where the volunteer, either alongside or collaborating with the chaplain or FFMPC program coordinator,[5] visits the patient/resident in their room or a private setting. The Four-Footed Ministerial team, in conjunction with the FFMPC program coordinator, interacts with that person, develops a relationship that provides the opportunity for the patient/resident to express their concerns and, if appropriate, prays or receives a blessing. Here is an example of the sequence of action that governs what happens in a one-on-one visit:

Visitation Sequence for Four-Footed Ministerial Team

1. Ask permission to enter the room or private area.
2. Identify yourself with your name, noting you are from the chaplain's office. Ask if person would like to visit with the dog.
3. If answer is yes, enter the room; if not, thank the person and wish them well.

---

[5] See Appendix B where there are two volunteer job descriptions. One describes the volunteer who wishes to work alongside the chaplain and/or Four-Footed Ministers Pastoral-Care program coordinator (FFMPC program coordinator). The second job description meets the needs of the volunteer who has sufficient training and experience in spiritual/pastoral care and wishes to work independently to a degree.

4. Encourage the resident to interact with the dog, listening deeply to their concerns and needs.
5. Ask if there is anything that the person needs or if they have concerns that should be addressed by spiritual/pastoral services.
6. End session with a blessing (if appropriate) wishing them well.

The following example of a verbatim provides the chaplain/director with an idea of how typical interactions develop. The characters are the spiritual/pastoral care provider (SPCP) and 'Mary,' a long-term care resident.

SPCP: Good morning, Mary. I am Jerilyn from the Sister Josephine's office. How are you doing today?

Mary: Well, Jerilyn, since I last saw you, I have been sick.

SPCP: I am sorry to hear that, Mary. I am so glad to see you today and you look like you are feeling better. Would you like to visit with Alya?

Mary: Yes.

SPCP: (brings the dog to the front of Mary's wheelchair so that Alya can lick her hand, as Mary is somewhat paralyzed and bent over). There, Alya is saying hello.

Mary (putting out her hand to be licked, and then begins petting Alya): Yes, she is. It is good to see you too, Alya.

SPCP: Does Sister know that you have not been well? Has anyone come to see you to bring you Holy Communion? So often many of our volunteers who bring communion to the sick can overlook someone if they are tucked back in their room or are asleep.

Mary: I haven't seen any volunteers or sisters lately. Would you tell Sister Josephine that I miss Holy Communion?

SPCP: Certainly. I will see Sister after completing our visiting rounds and I will let her know that you would like to be visited and receive communion.

Mary: That would be nice.

SPCP: Is there anything else?

Mary: I guess not.

SPCP: Well, we have to continue our rounds, Mary. Blessings!

Mary: Blessings to you also.

Within the CAM/PS model there is also the recognition of the importance of community prayer. Here both volunteer and spiritual/pastoral-care providers work in conjunction with the FFMPC program coordinator to gather and pray with a group. These dog ministry prayer-group gatherings are approximately 20-30 minutes in length and held in a community room or other gathering location. The chaplain or FFMPC program coordinator functions as a leader for the group by directing the participants through a process of theological reflection based on scriptures (not necessarily Christian), the attendees' own religious or spiritual tradition/orientation, and their own lived experience remembering their beloved pet(s). Based on a quality of the Divine that is illustrated by the sacred scripture reading and a question of how their pet illustrated that quality, each participant is invited to share stories about their interactions with their pet(s). The leader then asks how the insights from the stories might help each individual to come closer to God, the Divine, or a Higher Power.

Here is an outline of one such prayer service that was built around the quality of the compassion that God shows to His creatures:[6]

Four-Footed Ministers Pastoral-Care Program
Dog-Ministry Prayer-Group Gathering

Action	Script
Call to Prayer	With individuals seated in a circle: begin with "Let us all be in God's Spirit, and we begin this time of prayer and meditation in the name of the Holy One."
Silence	Time for centering and connecting to Spirit.
Welcome	"Welcome to the circle of wisdom where we can share our stories of our canine companions and other beloved animals. Today's lesson is that of compassion. "We begin with a mystery—a musty document has come across the desk of an academic who sees that it tells a story about Jesus not found in the Gospels. The story seems to answer the question, 'What if Jesus had a pet dog?' "This story is based on the method used by the rabbis in the Jewish tradition where they, being great storytellers who were filled with the Word of God, filled in the blanks left in the approved scripture stories. This story uses imagination to fill in those gaps left in the Gospel stories. "Since Jesus loved those who were outcasts from society, it seems logical that he would also take in outcasts from the animal world—dogs, for example. Dogs were outcast because they were scavengers and feasted on blood, an act that was forbidden according to the Jewish law. "What follows is a story about Jesus and a dog who found a place in the community of disciples. Our question for the day is, 'how did we show compassion toward our pet or another's animal when it was hurt or in trouble?' What does that tell us about God's compassionate care?"
Scriptural Reading	Read "Prologue" and "Chapter 1" of *The Master's Companion: A Christian Midrash*.[7] Adjust the amount read based on the situation at the time.
Silence	A period for reflection.
Faith-sharing time on compassion	Repeat the question of the day. Time for sharing of stories about past experiences where each resident has a chance to tell a story about their compassionate act toward an outcast animal.

---

[6] See Appendix C for a fuller exploration of this dog-ministry prayer-group gathering.

[7] Jerilyn E. Felton, *The Master's Companion: A Christian Midrash* (Winona, MN: St. Mary's Press, 2007).

Action	Script
Next Session*	"A Night in the Garden" (Chapter 2)—Jesus is our refuge from fear.
Conclusion: Sending Forth	"Let us now pray . . . Holy One, as we reflect on the beauty of your creation, let us takes the lessons we have learned into our community to spread Your joy, Your love, and Your peace. Amen."

*Note: At this juncture, individuals can be invited to hold up in prayer their own needs.

Both structures form the basis for the Four-Footed Ministers Pastoral-Care Program, as will be further explained in Unit Four. As this is an all-volunteer program, the time for individual visits and a schedule for the dog-ministry prayer-group gatherings should be carefully planned and have the possibility of being adjusted. The above structures provide an overall picture of the program's functioning.

The CAM/PS History

Shackleton wanted the crew to get exercise . . . . The dogs that had been brought along for pulling sleds were assigned to certain men for their care. Those men trained and bonded with those dogs and in this, maintained a real sense of purpose.[8]

In his book *Summoned to Lead*, Len Sweet uses the story of Sir Ernest Shackleton's trek to the South Pole as an example of how a leader hopes for the best but plans for the worst. When Shackleton and his crew were stranded, they found a way to survive by focusing on a purposeful activity: that of taking care of and bonding with the dogs that they brought with them. This story is an extreme example of how dogs can form important bonds to human beings regardless of their age or situation.

Perhaps an even more pointed story highlights the strong bond between the human and the dog, God's gift to the human being. In an anonymous *midrash* circulating on the Internet, God felt sorry for Adam, who had been banished from the Garden because of his sin. So, loving Adam very much, He created Dog. "And God said, 'Because I have created this new animal to be a reflection of my love for you, his name will be a reflection of my own name, and you will call him DOG.'"[9] Using dogs in ministry to elders required viewing the dog as *gift* and this perspective provided the real key for doing dog ministry.

As was mentioned, the idea for dog ministry was first formulated with a question: "How can a person take a dog to work when one begins working in ministry?" This question led to sketching a brief outline of a model for the integration of a canine companion into ministry to elders in a retirement community. A qualitative research study to test the model was conducted in June 2004 over a five-day period in a parish setting with independent elders who tested the group aspect of the model. The study was set up so that the volunteer subjects were read an animal-specific section taken from the scriptures of world religions,

---

[8] Leonard Sweet, *Summoned to Lead* (Grand Rapids, MI: Zondervan, 2004), 154.

[9] William Pollack and Fairfield Animal Hospital, "And God Created," http://www.phdproducts.com/main/phdpage.asp?page=149 (accessed April 15, 2010).

had time to ponder a question germane to a *quality* often attributed to God, and tell their pet story that demonstrated that quality and how this reflection might help them come closer to the Divine. The results generally supported the validity of the model accomplished through questionnaires where stories told became the backbone of the project. It appeared that this could be a fruitful line of study.

Recent examples of dogs in ministry originating from the secular press reveal that the idea of dog ministry is catching on. In July 2009, Erica Noonan of *The Boston Globe* wrote a human-interest article about the work of Mosby, the Ministry Dog, who visited the sick and nursing-care residents of his faith community in Littleton, Massachusetts. It was reported that the First Baptist Church welcomed Mosby for he, like a good dog, quietly curled up under a pew as services were conducted, but made himself available for interacting with the members of the congregation after services. He is acknowledged as an important part of the church community outreach.[10]

Even before Mosby came on the scene, Pet Partners®, a non-profit organization in Bellevue, Washington, had begun serious study of how dogs and other animals could benefit human beings. Over the course of several decades, Pet Partners® developed training curricula that offered volunteers and their dogs education in safety procedures to enable them to work in healthcare facilities. They could function as either "meet or greet" volunteer teams (animal-assisted activities) or work with professionals or paraprofessionals in the treatment of sick or injured individuals (animal-assisted therapy). As time progressed, Pet Partners® became a leader in recognizing and fostering research on the benefits of human interactions with dogs and other animals. Because of their rigorous work in the field, it was a natural step for Pet Partners® to develop a structure for registering pets and their owners. Healthcare facilities could then be confident that the Pet Partners®-registered teams would be knowledgeable about and take appropriate steps to ensure the safety of all participants when interacting with those who needed their care.

To provide a minimum standard for behavior, Pet Partners® developed a series of tests that were used to evaluate potential "therapy dogs." The tests evaluated the volunteers and their dogs as a team and this test structure provided a comprehensive way to evaluate how a team might perform in a healthcare setting. Pet Partners® has provided not only a training manual on the evaluation tests, but has also developed a series of standards for facilities that were interested in integrating "dog therapy" into their facility but had severe concerns about issues of safety and, just as importantly, liability.[11]

Beyond the Initial Discoveries—The Maryville Story

In the intervening years, work continued on the CAM/PS model. Though an increasing number of individuals had become interested in dog ministry, no one had yet developed a

---

[10] Erica Noonan, "A Dog with a Calling," *The Boston Globe*, July 16, 2009 under "/Your Town/ Medford," http://www.boston.com/yourtown/medford/articles/2009/07/16/as_a_ministry_dog_ littletons_mosby_brings_healing_touch_to_nursing_homes_and_hospitals/ (accessed January 26, 2012).

[11] Delta Society, *Standards of Practice: for Animal-Assisted Activities and Animal-Assisted Therapy* (Bellevue, WA: Delta Society, 1996).

road-tested, effective, safe, and repeatable program that could be used as a template for other unique programs. Thus, the CAM/PS model formed the basis for a doctoral qualitative research study that was conducted at Maryville Nursing Home, Beaverton, Oregon from May 2010 to May 2011. Here, the actual program was further refined and implemented, and has been sustained, demonstrating dog ministry in action (see Unit Two, The Maryville Nursing Home Story: Where the Program was Formulated).

Bibliography

Delta Society. *The Pet Partners® Team Training Course*. Bellevue, WA: Delta Society, 2008.

Delta Society. *Standards of Practice for Animal-Assisted Activities and Animal-Assisted Therapy*. Bellevue, WA: Delta Society, 1996.

Felton, Jerilyn E. "Four-Footed Ministers: A Roman Catholic Lay Pastoral Care Model for the Use of Canine Companions in Ministry to the Elderly in Retirement Communities." Marylhurst University, 2002.

_____. "Four-Footed Ministers: Their Theology of Presence—a Research Study on CAM/PS (Canine-Assisted Ministry/Pastoral and Spiritual Care)." Marylhurst University, 2005.

_____. *The Master's Companion: A Christian Midrash*. Winona, MN: St. Mary's Press, 2007.

Gammonley, Judith, and Judy Yates. "Pet Projects: Animal Assisted Therapy in Nursing Homes." *Journal of Gerontological Nursing* 17, no. 1 (1991): 12-15.

Johnson, Mary E., Dorothy Bell, Mary Eliot Crowley, and Katherine Piderman. "Mayo Clinic's Approach to Promoting Spiritual Research Reviewed." *Vision* 20, no. 4 (2010): 21-22.

Noonan, Erica. "A Dog with a Calling." *The Boston Globe*, July 16, 2009, "Your Town/Medford," http://www.boston.com/yourtown/medford/articles/2009/07/16/as_a_ministry_dog_ littletons_mosby_brings_healing_touch_to_nursing_homes_and_hospitals/ (accessed January 26, 2012).

Sweet, Leonard. *Summoned to Lead*. Grand Rapids, MI: Zondervan, 2004.

Pollack, William and Fairfield Animal Hospital. "And God Created." Phd Products. http://www.phdproducts.com/main/phdpage.asp?page=149 (accessed April 15, 2010).

UNIT TWO

THE MARYVILLE NURSING-HOME STORY: WHERE THE PROGRAM WAS FORMULATED

LESSON OVERVIEW:

This unit discusses the qualitative research project and its results, highlighting the stories of the people and dogs who made the Four-Footed Ministers Pastoral-Care Program work at Maryville during the nine-month study conducted between May 2010 and May 2011.

LESSON OBJECTIVES:

- ❖ To discover the story of the qualitative research study that defined the Four-Footed Ministers Pastoral-Care Program at Maryville.
- ❖ To appreciate the results of the study and provide preliminary questions that will help the chaplain/director of spiritual/pastoral care to determine the suitability of a Four-Footed Ministers Pastoral-Care Program for their healthcare facility.

The Maryville Nursing Home Story:
Where the Program Was Formulated

My doctoral mentor, James Wm. McClendon, Jr., taught me that the first task of theology is to locate our place in the story.[1]

Stories serve as a kind of mental map that helps people know, first, what is important (purpose and values) and, second, how things are done in a particular group or organization.[2]

Why do even the most educated of people tend to set aside their well-honed cynicism and critical nature when listening to a story? Because stories help individuals *transport themselves* away from the role of a listener who is rigorously applying rules of logic, analysis, and criticism and into the story itself.[3]

Stories are the powerful tools that the chaplain/director uses in spiritual/ pastoral-care interactions to understand the person before them.[4] The following pages provide the chaplain/ director with a glimpse into the qualitative study conducted at Maryville. In retelling the stories of the Maryville study participants, chaplains/directors can see the impact the Four-Footed Ministerial teams made on the study volunteers and those who just wanted to tell the human member of the team about their own beloved animal who was no longer permitted to be with them. It is an empirically demonstrated fact that the grief experience at "the loss of a pet can be as intense as the loss of a significant person, [and] the significance of pet loss is more likely to go unacknowledged."[5] The brief review given below begins with a discussion of the qualitative research design, including both the strengths and the limitations, and continues with the stories of how the interactions with the dogs made a difference in the spiritual lives of the study participants. This discussion concludes with a list of preliminary questions the chaplain/director should consider as that person thinks about a project to develop their own in-house Four-Footed Ministers Pastoral-Care Program.

---

[1]   Charles J. Conniry, Jr., *Soaring in the Spirit: Rediscovering Mystery in the Christian Life* (Colorado Springs, CO: Authentic Media, 2007), xiv.

[2]   James M. Kouzes and Barry Z. Posner, *The Leadership Challenge*, 3rd ed. (San Francisco: Jossey-Bass, 2002), 88.

[3]   Kerry Patterson, et. al, *Influencer: The Power to Change Anything* (New York: McGraw Hill Companies, 2008), 61 (italics theirs).

[4]   Rabbi Dayle A. Friedman, "PaRDes: A Model for Presence in *Hitlavut Rucharit*," In *Jewish Pastoral Care: A Practical Handbook from Traditional and Contemporary Sources* (Woodstock VT: Jewish Lights Publishing, 2001), 61.

[5]   Bruce S. Sharkin and Audrey S. Bahrick, "Pet Loss: Implications for Counselors," *Journal of Counseling & Development* 68, no. January/February (1990): 306.

The Qualitative Study at Maryville

The Research Design: The Informed-Consent Form

The thesis statement below summarizes both the history and the direction of the Maryville study and formed the lead paragraph for the informed-consent form that was presented to potential volunteers:

> Thesis Statement: Given the empirically demonstrated benefits of interactions of people with dogs, the CAM/PS model (canine-assisted ministry/pastoral and spiritual care) integrating canine-companions into pastoral care, took these beneficial animal-assisted interventions to the next level. In June 2004, the CAM/PS model was tried and affirmed as a viable way to connect independent elders in a parish setting through the process of theological reflection to God in a meaningful and beneficial way. In order to encourage use of the model in another setting and provide further development resulting in a program of spiritual/ pastoral care based on the CAM/PS model, this present study aims to set up an all-volunteer spiritual/pastoral-care provider program (Four-Footed Ministers Pastoral-Care Program) from which a training manual for directors of spiritual/pastoral care/services will be produced.

The informed-consent document continued to define risks and benefits for the potential volunteer in the study as the following paragraphs explained:

> At this point, there two areas that might be of concern. There is a risk of possible injury from the canine companion. On the personal/spiritual side, reminiscences about a beloved companion who has died might bring up unpleasant memories resulting in sadness and unexpressed grief.[6]
>
> While physical harm is a possible event, the researcher has tried to reduce the risk of injury by screening volunteers and their dogs for appropriate obedience training and behaviors. Each dog's health has been duly certified by a veterinarian as being up to date on shots and vaccinations. Each team will be required to have taken adequate flea control measures. All dogs will be Pet Partners® registered.
>
> With regard to the personal or spiritual stress that might arise from either one-on-one visits or prayer-group sessions, the social-services team is available to study participants to process any grief reactions. Realizing death is a part of the human condition and that our society does not honor grieving at the loss

---

[6] While the processing of pet loss became a very important theme in the June 2004 study, it did not figure prominently in the Maryville study (see Appendix A, Exhibit B, Notes on Pet Grief Support Gatherings at Maryville). However, one resident who was in hospice did process a loss of a pet with the researcher on a one-on-one basis. A hesitancy to discuss pet loss could be due to the limitation of time for visitation as well as the reluctance of the individuals involved to talk about the subject in a group, though the topic could have been important to the participants and could have been discussed in one-on-one visits.

of a pet, if memories of pet loss should arise, the social-services team and/or researcher will create a safe environment where this pet loss is acknowledged and supported.

The issue of confidentiality was outlined for the potential volunteer making the basic outline of the study complete:

> For individual visits, the Four-Footed Ministerial team will be accompanied by the researcher. Any stories deemed important to the research will be summarized in a written form and kept in a secure file. The researcher will make it possible for the participant to review this document at any time if allowing seven business days to process the request. The researcher will use a coding system to protect the participant's anonymity. The stories will remain in the files of the researcher.

The Research Design: The Elements of the Study

There were nine individuals (six women and three men) who were selected by the chaplain, the admissions coordinator, nursing staff, and senior staff. They were suggested as possible participants in the study because these long-term nursing-care residents had expressed a love of dogs, had cared for dogs in the past, and had no medical issues that would prevent them from participating. No one withdrew from the study, though one individual left the nursing home for adult foster-care (Dinah). One of the men (Seth) and one of the women (Deborah) died during the study. Each one of the potential volunteers had both the chaplain and researcher explain the study and each signed the informed consent form themselves or a healthcare representative signed it on their behalf.

One-on-one visits began in September 2010 and continued throughout the course of the study that concluded in May 2011. The one-on-one visits were attempted with all of the participants in order to build a level of trust with each person. Because of the compromised health condition of the participants who suffered from a variety of medical issues both physical and mental, it was often not possible to visit every week. Many of the residents were often not available for other reasons, such as outings arranged through the activities department that conflicted with the scheduled visitation time. Finally, the dogs, the two retired-Guide-Dog Labrador Retrievers used in the study, were very popular with visitors and other residents. It was often difficult to adhere to a formal schedule of visitation due to the many interruptions that occurred due to the nature of the open campus and the physical attraction of the dogs who looked like siblings; their presence always initiated questions from residents and visitors.[7]

---

[7] Marian R. Banks and William A. Banks, "The Effects of Group and Individual Animal-Assisted Therapy on Loneliness in Residents of Long-Term Care Facilities," *Anthrozoös* 18, no. 4 (2005): 398. In their article on a research study on AAT to reduce the effects of loneliness with residents in long-term care facilities, Marian R. Banks and William A. Banks mention the work of P. R. Messent (1983) who discovered that pet dogs could facilitate casual human encounters in a park. These encounters happened more frequently if the person their dog with them. The researcher's observations and experiences throughout the Maryville study confirmed this observation.

The test of the dog-ministry prayer-group-gathering structure began in January 2011, and group prayer was conducted on the same day as individual visits. Both modalities have continued beyond the conclusion of the study. It appeared from the regular attendance by study participants that dog-ministry prayer-group gatherings were more successful than the one-on-one interactions.[8] However, given the nature of spiritual/pastoral-care interactions where the "cornerstone of pastoral care" is the "comfort that can be given by simply 'being with' the sufferer," the issue of comfort rendered is increasingly important.[9]

One factor that could have contributed to the apparent success of the dog-ministry prayer-group gatherings was the fact that almost every human person likes a story. Using midrashic extension in exploring scripture and sacred story, many of the residents found these creative extensions to be fruitful ground in which to explore their relationship to God. The elements and process of theological reflection beginning with experience leading through self-awareness, the text, and finally to community were reversed in the case of dog-ministry prayer-group gatherings. An altered order was used in a research study conducted in 2004 and the Maryville study. Dog-ministry prayer-group began with a gathering of the community facilitated by the dog, then to a statement of a quality attributed to the Divine and a question, moving into the text, and ending with the experience revealed through the pet story. Given the variable presentness of each participant, the researcher found it best to move quickly but prayerfully through the dog-ministry prayer-group theological-reflection process. Ultimately, using a question based on a God-like quality often attributed to a pet, the participant could more readily see how their interactions with their pet, as revealed in their own story, could lead them to contemplate their relationship to God through that quality.[10] This theological reflection based in midrashic extension through pet stories provided a new potential avenue for the participants to access the meaning of the sacred text.[11] Midrashic extension provided an easy way in.

The Research Design: Strengths and Weaknesses

There were several areas where both strengths and weaknesses became evident as the study progressed. From the beginning, the study was to be a qualitative one, using interviews

---

[8] It is interesting to note that the researcher's observations are contrary to the results noted by Banks and Banks in the same study, 396-397. Though they attempted to build on their earlier study that indicated that AAT was beneficial to long-term care residents, Banks and Banks, in their 2005 study, found that AAT was more successful with individuals in reducing loneliness in one-on-one interactions rather than in the group. More research is needed in this area in order to determine if this is indeed consistent for dog-ministry prayer-group interactions.

[9] Rabbi Zahara Davidowitz-Farkas, "Jewish Spiritual Assessment," in *Jewish Pastoral Care: A Practical Handbook from Traditional and Contemporary Sources* (Woodstock, VT: Jewish Lights Publishing, 2001), 106.

[10] For more on the process of theological reflection see Anthony F. Krisak, "Theological Reflection: Unfolding the Mystery," in *Handbook of Spirituality for Ministers*, ed. Robert J. Wicks, vol. 1 (New York: Paulist Press, 1995), 310-325.

[11] For more information on the use of midrash as a pastoral-care tool in spiritual assessment see Davidowitz-Farkas, 107-108.

and observations from spiritual/pastoral-care interactions conducted in a one-on-one setting and in the group interactions. To begin with, there was no control group defined. This was due not only to the nature of the facility where the researcher was a "guest," but also because the aim of the study was the definition of a structure built on the CAM/PS model from which a training manual for chaplains/directors could be constructed. The lack of a control group is not unique. This same challenge had also been encountered in a study conducted by Ira Perelle and Diane Granville where they note that a lack of a control group did "dilute the strength of the results" and "because of the nature of the population and the institution, [an objective selection process and observations of a control group] were not possible."[12] Though a control group was lacking, this did not appear to significantly affect the outcome of the study, but points the way to further research refining the model.

As the aim of the study was to describe a structure for the Four-Footed Ministers Pastoral-Care Program, there was no formal baseline pre-test assessment taken. The selection of volunteers for the study was based on suggestions made by the staff. Their assessments depended on the individual's history of dog interactions or the resident's expressed wishes to participate. Therefore, the participants could be characterized as self-selected in this instance.

Finally, though the program appears to be a pioneer effort, the researcher did design and administer the oral assessment given at the end of the study to evaluate the research efforts (See Appendix A, Exhibit C). Though the questions were carefully reviewed and the researcher took every opportunity not to influence the answers given, it became apparent that the participants had developed a close relationship with her. This could have been a factor in the overwhelmingly positive results that came from the oral assessment. However, as the researcher is still involved in the program, positive comments about dog-ministry prayer-group gatherings have continued. Future studies would do well to use standardized assessment tools and external evaluators to determine the success of the model used in the program. However, in the final analysis, for a preliminary attempt at the formulation of a comprehensive structure for dog ministry, the study did prove successful in defining templates for a program using dogs in ministry.

---

[12] Ira Perelle and Diane Granville, "Assessment of the Effectiveness of a Pet-Facilitated Therapy Program in a Nursing-Home Setting," *Society Animals, Journal of Human-Animal Studies* 1, no. 1, http://www.societyandanimalsforum.org/sa/sa1.1/perelle.html (accessed November 26, 2011).

*Discussion: Glimpses of the Spiritual/Pastoral-Care Encounters
from One-on-One Visits and Dog-Ministry Prayer-Group Gatherings*

Following Rabbi Dayle Friedman's outline for understanding the human person, reading them like a book,[13] the first participant revealed that her dogs functioned as a lifeline for her, so administration permitted her to have one dog with her in her room. Staff recognized her connection to her companion dog and accommodated that dog's needs in the early months of her stay at Maryville. It became apparent that the dog meant more to her than just a companion, as the following story reveals:

> The issue of pet loss is the theme that runs through **Dinah's** story.[14] Dinah was a relatively young woman who had to give away one of her beloved dogs because she could only take one dog with her to Maryville. As it turned out, when she began to decline, the care of the dog fell to staff. It was then that the dog was adopted by a staff member.
>
> As a hospice patient, she wanted to participate in the study because, she said, it would give her a reason to live. In the initial interview, she related how her dogs gave her love and kisses when she got her terminal diagnosis that required her to move to Maryville. She remembered how they knew that something was wrong with their "mom" and they "licked away the tears" from her eyes.[15]
>
> As time progressed, she seemed to enjoy the visits with the FFM dogs and was always happy to see them. We were there for her and we always prayed with her, giving her a blessing as we were about to leave. Though she had times throughout that year when she rallied physically, the strain of not having a dog of her own began to weigh heavily on her. With outside help, she moved out of Maryville at the end of 2010 to a location where she could have a 'dog of her own.'

Another resident who loved dogs and appeared to have been somewhat isolated because of his declining health and relatively non-communicative stance revealed ever so slightly that dogs meant something to him beyond just a friendly face with whom to interact. He verbalized when around the dogs and came to dog-ministry prayer-groups if someone could bring him. He paid attention to the dogs when in the prayer group but seemed to be oblivious to other surroundings.

> **Seth** was another early participant in the study. He had been at Maryville for several years and, though appearing to suffer from a form of dementia, loved to interact with the dogs. The dogs always seemed to bring him out of himself to engage the world around him. He liked to have the dogs come to see him and would cluck at them to draw their attention.[16] Throughout the intervening months

---

[13] Friedman, "PaRDes," 61.

[14] Biblical names have been assigned for the study participants to further protect their identities.

[15] Chart notes: dated 7/18/2010. Stories quoted from chart notes will be noted by the date alone to protect the identity of the study participant.

[16] Chart notes: 9/17/2010.

of the study, he seemed to be withdrawing more completely into himself. Sister Josephine, the chaplain/director of spiritual services, mentioned in a debriefing session that Seth seemed to be very content with being alone in a sunny part of the facility processing his own thoughts.[17] In order to ensure that he could see the dogs, the staff assisted him in attending the dog-ministry prayer-group gatherings and he did so until the week before he died.

Joseph characterizes the other end of the spectrum with regard to engaging in life activities. **Joseph,** one of three men in the study, is a man who is always on the go despite his advancing years. Though a late riser, he seems to have a mental calendar and has many commitments within the facility, always cognizant of being there for his appointments. Because of his ability to get around by himself and because he enjoyed gathering with others, during the study he was a fixture of the dog-ministry prayer-group gatherings. He is a man whose mind has not dimmed with age. After one of the gatherings, Joseph told the following story about how close he felt to a friend's hunting dog:

> He told me [the researcher] about his experience of hunting with a friend's Vizsla. He thought that because the dog was used in hunting birds (killing them) some in our group might be upset by that issue so he decided to share this story privately with me. He said that remembering this dog "touched his button." I understood this to mean that it caused him to choke up with emotion because he pointed to his throat. He said how much he missed his hunting companion.[18] I tried to reassure him that there is a 'wideness in God's mercy' and that animals form a part of God's creation, side-stepping the issue of canine immortality. He seemed to be satisfied with that statement. [19]

This story reveals the deep attachment to and meaning of the dog to Joseph. Reminiscence was a very powerful tool in this instance, yet there seemed to exist an underlying sadness that future spiritual/pastoral-care encounters might illuminate.

---

[17] Chart notes: 12/16/2010.

[18] A pet-grief support group never seemed to come to fruition. See Exhibit B in Appendix A for the brief summaries concerning the efforts to start a group.

[19] Dog-ministry prayer-group gathering, dated 4/14/2011.

**A resident with Caterina and Alya
with Jerilyn in the background.**

The following stories of the women who were consistent study participants reveal the various challenges both physical and mental that were overcome as time progressed. Some had been faithful attendees at the dog-ministry prayer-group gatherings and others came as they could, depending on their feelings on that day. All were good friends who sat together at mealtimes and appeared to enjoy being together for the dog-ministry prayer-group gatherings that occurred outside of the normal daily liturgical offerings. Though each person's story could be interpreted differently depending on how the spiritual/pastoral-care person read the 'human document,' the stories below summarizing their engagement with the dogs helped expose something more about each person that normal spiritual/pastoral-care interactions might not have uncovered.

Jael's story tells us something of the facts of her life. She was a very sweet woman who had a severe physical challenge. Though confined to a wheelchair, she was always upbeat and seemed to be happy despite her lack of mobility. She loved to have the dogs visit her and loved to interact with them. She surprised the researcher by remembering Alya's name though she had not seen Alya for several weeks. The sisters who worked in her section needed to bring her to the dog-ministry prayer-group gatherings, but she came and seemed to enjoy her time together with her friends and the dogs. Though she did not share any special stories about dogs or cats, she seemed to be content to look at the dogs and be with them. Her interactions with the dogs gave her the opportunity to gather with others during the day other than at mealtimes. It appeared as if dog-ministry prayer-group gatherings were her avenue to community.

Deborah was the catalyst for the group of residents who ate meals together. She was always in the center of things. Moreover, she was computer savvy and loved to print out pictures of her friends that she had taken with her camera. She had a wonderful sense of humor that was illustrated in the following story:

Deborah was in her room and was wearing a tiara emblazoned with "2011." She was in a very festive mood, anticipating the New Year's Eve party that would be taking place on the following afternoon. As there were repairs being done in her part of the facility, there were several workmen moving about. They gravitated to Alya, who continued to lick Deborah's hand as we talked. Deborah mentioned that Alya "could not hold her licker." One of the workmen responded that she must not have her "licker license." We all got a great laugh out of that.[20] This dog-ministry visit had provided Deborah with another chance to showcase her great sense of humor.

Though Deborah's physical health was up and down over the course of the study, she seemed to be able to maintain her sense of humor. She had even ordered a set of kazoos for some of her mealtime buddies and was going to start a kazoo band. Unfortunately, she died before the kazoos she ordered arrived. At her memorial, led by her resident friends, her meal companions played those instruments in her memory.

A very stately woman named **Judith** had been a professional musician and was very elegant in her manners and her dress. She loved both of the dogs and loved to interact with them. She would use 'motherese' to talk to them just like a mother talks to her small child. She called Alya her "bootiful" baby.[21]

The dog-ministry prayer-group gathering seemed to be her favorite time to visit people and the dogs. She came to one of the early gatherings and stated that she loved the beginning of the story of *The Master's Companion*. When it came time for sharing, she offered her story of compassion for an animal by sharing with the group how the mutt she and her husband had adopted was a natural for ministry. This Four-Footed Minister mutt went with them to an "old folk's home" and greeted each person assembled appropriately and correctly without being taught how to interact. Judith told her story with excitement, for she was totally engaged in the process.

Abigail is a woman the Four-Footed Ministerial teams met when she was surrounded by her family, both local members and those visiting from out of town. Abigail loved to see Alya and Caterina but continued to mention "Caleb" whom we would later come to know more about. It turned out that Caleb was Abigail's cat who she would telephone every so often. She could not keep a pet at Maryville and her son had graciously agreed to take Caleb for her so she could keep in touch with him over the phone. She missed Caleb, though he "talked" to her weekly.[22]

---

20 Chart notes: date 12/30/2010.

21 Chart notes: 9/17/2010; 2/3/2011.

22 In her article about animals, Lynette A. Hart mentioned a study conducted by R. L. Zasloff and A. H. Kidd in 1994 that verified that those women who owned cats affirmed that cats gave them unconditional love and affection. The recognition of the importance of Caleb to Abigail confirms this observation. See Lynette A. Hart, "Positive Effects of Animals for Psychosocially Vulnerable

When the research team conducted a quick verbal assessment of the dog ministry one-on-one visits, Abigail was asked if the visits by the dogs had helped her spiritual life. She responded that she eagerly looked forward to the dogs visiting. She also mentioned that she had noticed how several of her friends who were ill had been helped by the 'dog visits.'[23]

The final woman in the study was **Sarah,** a woman with a wealth of stories about her lifetime of interactions with both dogs and cats. In the dog-ministry prayer-group gatherings, Sarah shared stories about her animals. One story particularly stood out because it reflects the general feeling that married couples have about their dogs.

Sarah shared with us her joy of being able to take her dog, Maura, a black poodle, with her into the surf when she visited the beach. Though the dog picked up sand and sea in her coat, creating a bit of a mess to clean up, Sarah enjoyed being with her and mentioned briefly about the stillness and quiet she had experienced. Further, Sarah recalled an interchange she had with her late husband of 25 years when he lamented that she loved the dog more than she loved him; she responded, "I'm sorry you noticed."

A resident with Sister Josephine, Barbara, Caterina, Alya and Jerilyn.

People," in *Handbook on Animal-Assisted Therapy: Theoretical Foundations and Guidelines for Practice*, ed. Aubrey H. Fine (San Diego: Academic Press, 2010), 64.
[23]   Chart notes: 12/16/2010.

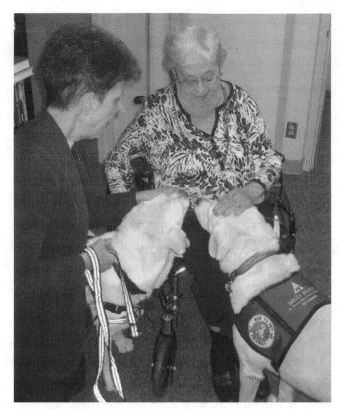

A study participant with Jerilyn, Alya, and Caterina.

The final male participant in the study falls into a class by himself because of the nature of the helping profession he had exercised during his working life. He had been involved in church work, but the animals who had graced his life were very important to him, as his reminisces about the family dog revealed.

Sean had been a clergyman and enjoyed being with dogs throughout his entire life. He is a real storyteller, relating stories about his beloved Kerry Blue Terrier, Mike, a dog he had as a child. Because he came from a large family, Sean noted that Mike often wanted to get away from the family and would hide out so that he could get some peace.

In November 2010, Sean was very excited because he was going to have the chance to use his ministry background for a Bible-study gathering. Unfortunately, he had a physical setback toward the end of the month so could not conduct the gathering.

As time went on, Sean enjoyed coming to the dog-ministry prayer-group gatherings if he could get there. His condition required that one of the CNAs bring him or accompany him as he used his walker. He made it to several of the gatherings, offering a blessing at the conclusion of one of them and, most importantly, when blessing a group he never forgot the dogs.

In the final analysis, the research study points to the following challenges that a chaplain/director should seriously consider when thinking about how they might set up and implement a Four-Footed Ministers Pastoral-Care Program in their facility:

- ❖ The research revealed that many of the impromptu interactions within a hallway or on the way to a patient/resident's room presented opportunities for both residents and visitors to engage the Four-Footed Ministerial teams. Normally these individuals connected to the dogs first, then related their dog stories to the human counterpart. Unfortunately, these impromptu visits often prevented the teams from attending to those who had scheduled visits. (See Appendix A, Exhibit B, Notes on General Visitation).
- ❖ A weakness not previously mentioned relates to the issue of a consistent gathering location for the dog-ministry prayer-group gatherings. Though the stories do not reveal this, the assignment of a particular place would have helped to create a sense of schedule and predictable routine for the participants, especially given the fact that many depended on CNAs to bring them to the group. Areas that were thought to be ideal for a gathering did not work out because of scheduling difficulties with the activities department. From experiences beyond the study, it was discovered that meeting in the same place every week has made a tremendous difference in aiding residents to come to the group.
- ❖ The research revealed that the time for scheduling visits did not work with the residents' schedules. It was necessary for the teams to change their visitation day from Fridays, when activities outside the facility were often scheduled, to Thursdays from 10 a.m. to noon, when most residents were available. Given the two-hour-per-day visitation window for the dogs, as required by Pet Partners® protocols, timing issues have become important considerations in scheduling both individual visits and dog-ministry prayer-group gatherings.
- ❖ One additional challenge that the research uncovered was the necessity to ask staff to assist with gathering the residents for dog-ministry prayer-group gatherings. Many of the residents would have liked to attend, but often did not remember the time designated for the gathering or know the place where the gatherings were being held. Sister Josephine was instrumental in making sure that those who wanted to come were able to gather in prayer with the dogs.
- ❖ The research confirmed that the chaplain/director is often required to put forth extra effort in publicizing and helping facilitate an effective gathering. Sister Josephine was normally apprised of the scriptural reading for the week and she prepared handouts of that scriptural piece for those who were still able read. She made sure that there was a sign posted to notify all residents where and at what time we were to gather. She even arranged the physical space to make it more inviting to the participants who were in wheelchairs.
- ❖ Finally, the research study confirmed the wisdom of visiting in pairs. The researcher and her ministry partner felt that they were more successful in their one-on-one visits as well as their group interactions if both teams could be present, even though this decreased the number of possible visits.

The above results define some of the successes and challenges encountered in the Maryville study. The subsequent chapters will assist the chaplain/director in discovering what makes up the Four-Footed Ministers Pastoral-Care Program and how this program might provide comfort and spiritual/pastoral care for their patients/residents.

Preliminary Personal and Facility-Analysis Questions

The following provides the chaplain/director with questions that will aid in a preliminary assessment of one's personal commitment and the facility's willingness to accommodate a Four-Footed Ministers Pastoral-Care Program. Helpful resources and suggestions as to answers to these questions will follow in the subsequent chapters:

1. Am I willing to take on the additional duties required by the program?[24]
2. Will I be willing to present the program to administration and infection control?
3. Are there potential challenges with regard to staff members who might be allergic to dogs or afraid of them? Would a short survey of the nursing staff and CNAs be in order as I consider implementing the program?
4. Am I able to educate myself to the point where I can make an informed decision as to who might function in the role of FFMPC program coordinator? Are there individuals who can assist me in this endeavor?
5. Is the facility able to accommodate dog visitations?[25]
6. Will the activities department be willing to work with the Four-Footed Ministerial teams who call on patients/residents?
7. Is there a time slot where dog-ministry prayer-group gatherings can be scheduled so that prayer does not conflict with other activities going on in the facility?
8. Is there a place that can be easily accessible to patients/residents where the dog-ministry prayer-group gatherings can be held on a consistent basis?

Bibliography

Banks, Marian R. and William A. Banks. "The Effects of Animal-Assisted Therapy on Loneliness in an Elderly Population in Long-Term Care Facilities." *Journal of Gerontology: Medical Sciences 2002* 57A, no. 7, (2002) M428-M432.

_____. "The Effects of Group and Individual Animal-Assisted Therapy on Loneliness in Residents of Long-Term Care Facilities." *Anthrozoös* 18, no. 4, (2005) 396-408.

Conniry, Jr., Charles J. *Soaring in the Spirit: Rediscovering Mystery in the Christian Life.* Colorado Springs, CO: Authentic Media, 2007.

---

24 See Appendix B: Program Forms-Exhibit A that lists the additional duties.

25 Flooring issues such as tile versus carpet will need to be considered in planning how the program unfolds. Physical-plant issues such as potty areas, areas that allow the dogs to take breaks, etc., are important considerations at the beginning planning stages.

Friedman, Rabbi Dayle A., ed. *Jewish Pastoral Care: A Practical Handbook from Traditional and Contemporary Sources.* Woodstock, VT: Jewish Lights Publishing, 2001.

Davidowitz-Farkas, Rabbi Zahara. "Jewish Spiritual Assessment." In *Jewish Pastoral Care,* 104-124.

Friedman, Rabbi Dayle A. "PaRDeS: A Model for Presence in Hitlavut Ruchanit." In *Jewish Pastoral Care,* 60-73.

Hart, Lynette A. "Positive Effects of Animals for Psychosocially Vulnerable People: A Turning Point for Delivery." In *Handbook on Animal-Assisted Therapy: Theoretical Foundations and Guidelines for Practice.* Edited by Aubrey H. Fine, 59-84. San Diego, CA: Academic Press, 2010.

Kouzes, James M., and Barry Z. Posner. *The Leadership Challenge.* San Francisco: Jossey-Bass, A Wiley Company, 2002. Reprint, 3rd.

Krisak, Anthony F. "Theological Reflection: Unfolding the Mystery." In *Handbook of Spirituality for Ministers*, edited by Robert J. Wicks, 308-329. vol. 1. New York: Paulist Press, 1995.

Patterson, Kerry, Joseph Grenny, David Maxfield, Ron McMillan, and Al Switzler. *Influencer: The Power to Change Anything.* New York: McGraw Hill Companies, 2008.

Perelle, Ira B. and Diane A. Granville, "Assessment of the Effectiveness of a Pet Facilitated Therapy Program in a Nursing Home Setting." Society and Animals Forum, Inc. http://www.societyandanimalsforum.org/sa/sa1.1/perelle.html (accessed November 26, 2011)

Sharkin, Bruce S., and Audrey S. Bahrick. "Pet Loss: Implications for Counselors." *Journal of Counseling & Development* 68, no. January/February (1990): 306-308.

UNIT THREE

FORMATION PROCESS OF BUILDING A CULTURE OF SERVICE

LESSON OVERVIEW:

This unit will present a schema concentrating on a spiritual-formation process that builds on a culture of service.

LESSON OBJECTIVES:

- ❖ To learn about a process of spiritual formation that taps already existing cultural components latent within the notion of service rendered to others.
- ❖ To appreciate the contributions made by each segment of the populations involved in the nursing-home environment that creates the culture of service and care.
- ❖ To intentionally engage these populations to appreciate their gifts for spiritual/pastoral care to each other through working with volunteer Four-Footed Ministerial teams.

Lesson 3.1: Religious/Ministerial Formation Schema

To understand the populations that make up a nursing-home environment, both ministerial and clinical documents can provide insight into the complex organism that is called 'human.' A work on lay-ecclesial ministry published by the United States Conference of Catholic Bishops entitled *Co-Workers in the Vineyard of the Lord*[1] treats the human being from a perspective of the human, intellectual, spiritual, and pastoral dimensions. These dimensions interact through the formation process so that ministers can carry out their ministerial duties more effectively. These four areas dovetail with the clinical division of therapeutic goals defined by Dr. Judy Gammonley in her article entitled, "Animal-Assisted Therapy as a Modality within Nursing."[2] Here, she set up a sample nursing plan using animal-assisted therapy. Both schemas can be utilized when considering how to tap into the already-present culture of service that should be operational in a nursing-home environment.

While the descriptor 'human' can be seen as incorporating the physical and the cognitive, the description of physical and cognitive goals in Gammonley's sample nursing-treatment plan point to activities that the patient/resident is encouraged to perform to bring about their healing. In the realm of ministry formation, the human, intellectual, spiritual, and pastoral dimensions also outline intentional activities the lay minister undertakes to become more formed in the image of Christ for the good of other human beings.[3] Thus, both sets of descriptors point to intentional activity to be undertaken for a specific purpose of healing or more effective ministry.

The last two goals Gammonley mentioned in her sample nursing plan were psycho-social and spiritual. With the aid of a therapy animal, activities in these areas helped the individual seeking healing in connecting to community. Further, these activities have the potential to assist that individual through contact with the animal to enter a new plane of reality. Gammonley mentioned, quoting from an earlier article, that the 'spiritual' was one of the five categories where animal-assisted therapy was appropriate for healing.[4] She quoted a study by L. Nebbe where the spiritual response is defined as one where "an animal provides a sense of oneness with creation and a sense of well-being. Hospice patients renew their spiritual energy through reminiscence. This activity takes place by daily interactions with the resident cat [used in her study] and/or staff. A sense of well-being occurs while holding the cat."[5] This is a good start, but these interactions can be seen as meaning so much more than this, as was demonstrated in the stories of the study participants described in Unit Two.

---

[1] United States Conference of Catholic Bishops, ed. *Co-Workers in the Vineyard of the Lord: A Resource for Guiding the Development of Lay Ecclesial Ministers*, vol. Publication No. 5-724 (Washington, D. C.: USCCB Publishing, 2005). See Part Two, Section B where the specifics of formation in the four areas are discussed at length from a formation viewpoint.

[2] Judy Gammonley, "Animal-Assisted Therapy as a Modality within Nursing," in *Animal-Assisted Therapy: Therapeutic Interventions* (Bellevue, WA: Delta Society, 1997), 5-6.

[3] M. Robert Mulholland, Jr., *Invitation to a Journey: A Road Map for Spiritual Formation* (Downers Grove, Ill: InterVarsity Press, 1993), 12.

[4] Gammonley, "Animal-Assisted Therapy," 2.

[5] Ibid.

In understanding the nursing-home culture as formative, the formation process itself can be thought of as a molding procedure that takes place within the human person because that person resides within a physical, social, cultural, and spiritual world.

> Everything influences the human person in this world, for, every thought we hold, every decision we make, every action we take, every emotion we allow to shape our behavior, every response we make to the world around us, every relationship we enter into, every reaction we have toward the things that surround us and impinge upon our lives—all of these things, little by little, are shaping us into some kind of being.[6]

The human being has no choice in the matter of being shaped[7] into some new being dictated by these factors in their surroundings. Thus, each facility would do well to examine how their environment lives up to their commitment to provide caring service to those who cannot care for themselves.

If the nursing-home culture is such an important part of formation for all those who interact within it, then what does the environment within the facility look like and how can the aspects of spiritual formation be undertaken for the benefit of the whole community?

Lesson 3.2: Populations in Spiritual Formation

By its very nature, a nursing-home facility should be a place that provides skilled nursing care to individuals who are incapacitated by injury, sickness, and/or old age. The creation of a caring environment depends on its people as well as its physical plant. It is the quality of loving service, 'ministry' in the best sense of the word, which can be the formational element to be used by the chaplain/director to their advantage when looking at the formation process within their facility.

Looking at Staff

As staff members from the senior level down review interactions that create community, the environment of the facility can take on aura of ministry. The chaplain/director can be aware, through observation, whether or not a caring environment exists. He or she can notice the interactions of staff members with patients/residents to help those staff members become aware of the fact that their work not only impacts the individual they have before them, but also those who surround them, such as family members or visitors. According to the current pontiff, "A respectful and compassionate silence, a prayerful presence, a gesture of tenderness and comfort, a kind look, a smile, often achieve more than many words."[8]

---

[6]   Mulholland, *Invitation to a Journey*, 23.

[7]   Ibid.

[8]   Benedict XVI, "Sickness," in *Spiritual Thoughts Series,* (Washington, D. C.: United States Conference of Catholic Bishops, October, 2010), par. 69.

Staff meetings are a good time to alert the nursing staff and CNAs to the importance of their interactions with patients/residents, family members, and visitors. Repetition of the facility's mission statement can be helpful in re-affirming the purpose for their work. The mission statement that guides the work at Maryville is the simple proclamation of "Service with Love." It is the driving force behind the work they do. Awareness and affirmation of the mission are two activities that take little time, yet pay big dividends.

Looking at Patients/Residents

In his booklet entitled "Sickness," the current pontiff, Benedict XVI, puts the diminishment experienced by patients/residents into perspective. He states,

> In our generation, in our culture, we have to rediscover the value of suffering in general, and we have to learn that suffering can be a very positive reality which helps us to mature, to become more ourselves, and to be closer to the Lord who suffered for us and suffers with us.[9]

Though this is written from a Roman Catholic point of view, the acknowledgement of the reality of suffering and the unity of all sentient beings, coupled with the ache to relieve that suffering, is echoed throughout the scriptures and traditions of world religions. For both those who profess to be Christians and those who follow a non-Christian faith tradition, such encouragement from this religious leader gives them hope that their suffering has meaning and purpose. Finally, it can be said that the above sensibility is not just a concept that informs a 'believer's' perspective alone, but is one that can also inform those who profess to be spiritual-but-not-religious.

There are many more individuals in this current day who come to nursing homes professing to be spiritual-but-not-religious. They have a profoundly deep spiritual connection to the Divine. Though the chaplain/director might profess a certain faith tradition, the sense of caring compassion on the human and pastoral level will be felt and appreciated by those who are in need of spiritual care. In most cases, a compassionate act will be received as such by most individuals, who will recognize the caring concern that flows from actions that may be performed in the name of a Christian God, though the Divine is not named.

The spiritual-not-religious person who likes dogs and readily interacts with them on a purely human level will respond to ministerial attempts at spiritual care in their own spiritual way. This may not be immediately apparent to the Four-Footed Ministerial team. Thus, interactions by the team with this individual should affirm and support that person whose sensibilities are not conformed to a particular religious tradition. In the end, the lead must always be directed by the patient/resident. Regardless of the patient/resident's belief or non-belief, the spiritual care of the spiritual-but-not-religious persons in the nursing-home population must be acknowledged and affirmed, especially by those who minister to them.

It must be noted that within the realm of the pastoral dimension, many believers and non-believers, including the spiritual-but-not-religious, do not see the important role they play in the spiritual formation of those who serve them. From a purely human standpoint, it

---

[9]   Ibid., par. 28.

is important that patients/residents be thought of as being part of the spiritual/pastoral-care service team. They provide their care in the form of being open to receiving the gifts of service from the staff as well as the Four-Footed Ministerial teams who visit. In this instance, their contribution cannot be understated. Their openness to receive is essential in the creation of a loving community of care and service needed for a nursing-home facility to totally fulfill its mission.

Looking at the Four-Footed Ministerial Teams

Building on Pet Partners® protocols that define animal-assisted therapy to be a volunteer team working in conjunction with a professional or paraprofessional to accomplish measurable therapeutic goals, it became apparent from the Maryville study that two types of job descriptions for Four-Footed Ministerial teams would be necessary. As those with pastoral-care training or extensive spiritual/pastoral-care experience might not necessarily need the visitation support of the chaplain and/or FFMPC program coordinator, it became necessary to create a separate job description for those volunteers who did need that support. Thus, a job description designated as "volunteer" was created. This type of volunteer role paralleled the function of a Pet Partners® team used in animal-assisted therapy (see Appendix B, Program Forms, Four-Footed Ministers Pastoral-Care Program, volunteer). This job description makes orientations in volunteer procedures and basic pastoral-care awareness required; however, further training in spiritual/pastoral care is optional. After some time working as a "volunteer", that individual may wish to obtain additional spiritual/ pastoral-care training to enable that person to be evaluated for solo visits.

The spiritual-care provider (see Appendix B Program Forms, Four-Footed Ministers Pastoral-Care Program, spiritual-care provider) is an individual who has had spiritual/ pastoral-care training or extensive experience in pastoral care such as an ordained member of a faith community or an individual who has completed one or more units of Clinical Pastoral Education. Because of this extensive training, this individual is able to visit patients/residents solo or paired with the FFMPC program coordinator and will be required to document their visits for the chaplain/director in the Four-Footed Ministers Assessment Tool form (see Appendix B, Exhibit J: Sample of Four-Footed Ministers Assessment Tool). Any concerns noticed will be recorded so that the chaplain/director can attend to them or, if appropriate, record them in the patient/resident's chart.

The linchpin of the Four-Footed Ministers Pastoral-Care Program is the program coordinator (see Appendix B Program Forms, Four-Footed Ministers Pastoral-Care Program, program coordinator). This person has had training in both worlds: working or training in spiritual/pastoral care[10] as well as working with Pet Partners®-registered dogs. This individual works under the supervision of the chaplain/director, collaborating closely with that individual in running the program. Depending on the requirements of the facility, this individual is responsible for scheduling visiting teams, handling paperwork for the teams, and working with teams as the chaplain/director dictates. In conjunction with the

---

[10]   To fulfill the spiritual/pastoral-care requirement, the successful candidate should possess either CPE training, be ordained in their faith tradition, or possess a graduate certificate in pastoral care.

chaplain/director, this individual helps to train staff and volunteers as to the specifics of the program. At Maryville, the FFMPC program coordinator works with the volunteer coordinator in updating the *Maryville Volunteer Handbook* to ensure that the section on the Four-Footed Ministers Pastoral-Care Program is current.

Spiritual formation with the spiritual-care provider is more highly structured because of the nature of their volunteer service. Therefore, training in spiritual/pastoral-care issues, opportunities for debriefing sessions with the chaplain/director, and attention to prayer and spiritual formation within their own faith community are required. Formal prayer sessions could be scheduled for these volunteers as their numbers within the facility increase.

This section has described an overarching schema for spiritual formation using both religious and clinical sources that describe the possibilities for formation latent in the nursing-home culture itself. These unrecognized forces define areas where spiritual formation can arise organically. With the structure of job descriptions for the two types of volunteers as well as the job description for the Four-Footed Ministers Pastoral-Care program coordinator, the chaplain/director is well on their way to developing their own in-house program based on these templates found in Appendix B. The next unit lays out more program specifics for the Four-Footed Ministers Pastoral-Care Program.

Checklist for Chaplains

- ❖ Awareness and affirmation of the mission: are these being acknowledged and confirmed in staff meetings?
- ❖ Has the willingness to receive the service of others by patients/residents been acknowledged as important to the creation of a culture of spiritual/pastoral care?
- ❖ How many spiritual-but-not-religious patients/residents reside in the facility? Are their spiritual needs being met?
- ❖ Will the Four-Footed Ministerial teams have adequate support and follow-up to their work by either the chaplain/director or the FFMPC program coordinator?

Bibliography

Benedict XVI. "Sickness." In *Spiritual Thoughts Series*. Washington, D. C.: United States Conference of Catholic Bishops, October, 2010.

Gammonley, Judy. "Animal-Assisted Therapy as a Modality within Nursing." In *Animal-Assisted Therapy: Therapeutic Interventions*. Bellevue, WA: Delta Society, 1997.

Mulholland, Jr., M. Robert. *Invitation to a Journey: A Road Map for Spiritual Formation*. Downers Grove, Ill: InterVarsity Press, 1993.

United States Conference of Catholic Bishops, ed. *Co-Workers in the Vineyard of the Lord: A Resource for Guiding the Development of Lay Ecclesial Ministers*. Vol. Publication No. 5-724. Washington, D. C.: USCCB Publishing, 2005.

UNIT FOUR

THE FOUR-FOOTED MINISTERS PASTORAL-CARE PROGRAM

LESSON OVERVIEW:

This unit will discuss the 'nuts and bolts' of the Four-Footed Ministers Pastoral-Care Program, providing the chaplain/director with a look at more program elements to help them to ascertain the feasibility and possible development of an in-house program for their facility.

LESSON OBJECTIVES:

- ❖ To learn how the components of the program are designed, operate, and interface with one another through a theology of presence and touch.
- ❖ To come to an appreciation the importance of the program as a conduit for spiritual comfort and care for those within the facility.

Lesson 4.1: Administrative Duties of the FFMPC Program Coordinator: Where It's All About Relationship

Within any healthcare facility, there is a division of labor that requires all departments to work toward fulfillment of the organization's mission. As Maryville has the mission of providing "Service with Love," the Four-Footed Ministers Pastoral-Care Program has become an asset to the facility by enhancing the service of the spiritual/pastoral care department in the areas of internal and external community relationships.[1]

Currently, this program is an all-volunteer effort and has had little or no direct financial impact on the facility. It is possible that at some future time, the program might evolve to the point where the volunteer FFMPC program coordinator will become a paid member of the staff because of the increased workload due to an expanded number of visitation teams as well as the possibility of the assumption of additional volunteer supervisory duties. The FFMPC program coordinator functions as the liaison between the various departments of nursing care, activities, and spiritual care, advocating on behalf of the patients/residents and the volunteer Pet Partners® teams. These efforts have already resulted in a perception of care and concern both internally and externally.

As the main focus of the FFMPC program coordinator is administration of the program, this person assists department heads to understand the benefits of the program and calm the fears of those who could perceive the program as an encroachment to their areas of influence. Thus, facility cultural sensitivity is of vital importance for the person who fills this role, especially as this person is currently a volunteer and not a staff member.

As the program administrator, the FFMPC program coordinator (see Appendix B: Program Forms, Exhibit B) works under the direct supervision of the chaplain/director. The job description for the FFMPC program coordinator defines the following administrative duties that are crucial to the running of the program:

- ❖ Maintain file of health records on dogs in the program;
- ❖ Develop health requirements for FFM teams based on good practices for animal-assisted interventions;
- ❖ Maintain FFM pastoral-care log file for program;[2]
- ❖ Register and credential FFM teams for visitation;
- ❖ Schedule volunteer FFM teams for one-on-one visitation;
- ❖ Schedule (and prepare) prayer-group gatherings with activities department;[3]

---

[1] Early in the study, the chaplain informed the author that there had been a donation made to Maryville specifically because the donor had noticed that there were dogs working within the facility.

[2] Rev. Richard B. Gilbert, "Chaplains and Charting," *Healing Ministry* 17, no. 3 (2011): 11-13. In the study at Maryville, charting was supplanted by debriefing sessions after visitation/group ministry. If items of concern did arise, they were discussed with the chaplain at that time. She determined if the information should be charted.

[3] For the Maryville Study, the program was run independently of the activities department. Because it was a study and not generally open to those outside of the study participants, coordination problems resulted with regard to a consistent meeting space and time. However, these were handled as they arose. Moreover, the FFMPC program coordinator was responsible for preparing

- ❖ Schedule FFM team in-services and continuing-education sessions for staff and volunteers;
- ❖ Assign volunteers to residents who request one-on-one visits;[4]
- ❖ Be responsible for supplies for dogs kept in the volunteer office;
- ❖ Update *Maryville Volunteer Handbook* section on FFM teams as needed;[5]
- ❖ Develop and modify forms for the program.

Based on the above duties, during the study, the FFMPC program coordinator devoted between two and four hours per week to these tasks. This volunteer time was allocated between on-site visitation and work done at home. As there was only one other volunteer team involved in the Maryville study (Barbara Miller and Caterina), scheduling visitations and group gatherings did not present an insurmountable obstacle. As more teams are recruited and more patients/residents are added to the list for visitation, more time will have to be allotted to this position. *As a preliminary requirement for participation, it is imperative that every team that works in the Four-Footed Ministers Pastoral-Care Program be Pet Partners®-registered and have up-to-date credentials.*

Though Maryville is a relatively open campus, there were visitation documents designed and used at the beginning of the study (see Appendix B, Program Forms, Exhibits I and J for examples). However, the use of these was abandoned after a time because it became evident that debriefing sessions with the chaplain/director were more productive. Sample forms are provided to enable larger programs to have an adequate way to document volunteer visits. These examples are easily modified to meet the level of expertise of the chaplain and/or volunteers. Their use will result in the effective implementation and maintenance of the program.

Lesson 4.2: One-On-One Visits: The Theology of Presence and Touch

"The elderly should not be reduced to remembering the way it felt to be touched."[6] This statement encapsulates the current cultural state of affairs with regard to those who are in compromised health and find themselves in a nursing-home facility. It is truly unfortunate that both the presence and the touch of one human being reaching out to another is becoming a thing of the past. "The twenty-first century is increasingly being asked to live without touch."[7] One can see that the massive use of technology has distanced person from person, for as

---

the weekly dog-ministry prayer-group gathering and this duty continues to be part of her responsibilities. The problem of a consistent gathering space was solved by Sister Josephine through her action of reserving a small reception area for the weekly gatherings.

[4] Because the study was small, there was no need to make any formal assignments, though staff did contact the FFMPC program coordinator if a patient/resident requested a visit.

[5] This responsibility could be negotiable depending on the requirements of the facility.

[6] Leonard Sweet, *Nudge: Awakening Each Other to the God Who's Already There* (Colorado Springs, CO: David C. Cook, 2010), 245.

[7] Ibid., 240.

technology increases, physical touch decreases.[8] Technological interaction, such as texting and email, is a poor substitute for contact with a living, breathing being who is focused and responsive to another.

Added to this is the fact that, with the bulk of the population aging, nursing-home staff is asked to do more with less. The number of caregivers appears to be decreasing while the number of those needing care increases. This leads to situations where elders are more likely to be handled as a commodity rather than touched lovingly.[9] While this lack of mindfulness is part of the human condition, the pressure to help and assist patients/ residents within a limited time frame often leads to forgetfulness of the holy work that the staff member performs for those who cannot do for themselves.

The Four-Footed Ministers Pastoral-Care Program provides a way for this lack of presence and acceptable touch to be overcome through the appreciation of the 'self-gift' of a dog.[10] Dogs will reach out for those drawn to them by allowing the human to pet them or by licking an outstretched hand.[11] In the American culture, touching a dog is culturally acceptable by either a male or female and is, in our dog-crazy world, encouraged. Therefore, an important spiritual connection can be made through the dog because the dog is both present and touchable. This bridge of connectivity can be encouraged and built upon as visits continue and relationships develop, eventually moving the connection from the physical plane alone to both the physical and spiritual planes. "The dog is always more than we know, extending beyond our knowledge, and calling on us to match its excess with acts of generosity of our own."[12]

Lesson 4.3: Dog-Ministry Prayer-Group Gatherings

As loneliness seems to increase as one ages, the gathering of community becomes more and more important, because "pets, otherwise known as 'companions,' alleviate the stress and alienation of old age and illness."[13] This is where animal-assisted therapy has empirically demonstrated that feelings of loneliness are reduced in those elders who wish to participate in

---

8   Ibid., 246.

9   Jerilyn E. Felton, "'If I but Touch the Hem of His Cloak . . .': 'Touching Prayer' as the Best of Both Worlds," *Healing Ministry* 13, no. 3 (Summer 2006). This article provides ways busy staff can make their work a prayer.

10   Stephen H. Webb, "Pet Theories: A Theology for the Dogs," *Soundings* 78, no. 2 (Summer 1995): 214.

11   The Maryville study confirmed that licking, a perceived fault in a therapy dog, was an asset to ministry work with elders. Many elders could not, because of the nature of their infirmity, interact with a dog unless that dog first extended herself to them through the process of licking. This was very powerfully illustrated in an instance where a patient/resident was unable to communicate or touch the ministry dog unless an aid assisted the person to extend a hand. The dog's licking of the person's hand caused visible joy to that physically challenged person observable to all in the room.

12   Webb, "Pet Theories," 230-231.

13   Salvatore Giaquinto and Fabio Valentini, "Is There a Scientific Basis for Pet Therapy?" *Disability and Rehabilitation* 31, no. 7 (2009): 598.

this type of interaction.[14] It appears that the dog seems to bring people together by its nature for those willing to be a part of a community. Therefore, group gatherings integrating dogs, having a spiritual/pastoral care goal, are a natural extension of the one-on-one connection.

In the Maryville study, it became apparent that when the dogs (two Four-Footed Ministers) entered the building, they were immediately the center of attention for eager elders and their family members excited to interact with them. Throughout the study, the individuals would seek to touch or otherwise interact with the dogs, often moving beyond the human component of the Four-Footed Ministerial team directly to the dogs. Some individuals were happy to sit back and just look at the dogs that looked so very much alike they could almost be sisters. In any case, the dogs constantly drew a crowd as soon as they came into the building.

From left to right: Alya and Jerilyn;
Caterina and Barbara.

A sample of a dog-ministry prayer-group gathering is provided in Appendix C, defining the various sequences of actions that make up prayer gatherings. It is important to note that while the dogs are present and are able to be touched, they should not be the focus of the gathering. The dogs in the Maryville study were on long leads and able to interact with those who called to them, as they were usually placed in the center of the prayer circle so that they

---

14   Marian R. Banks and William A. Banks, "The Effects of Animal-Assisted Therapy on Loneliness in an Elderly Population in Long-Term Care Facilities," *Journal of Gerontology: Medical Sciences*, vol. 57A, no. 7: M431.

were visible and touchable. Some residents who participated did tend to focus more on the dogs than the prayer.[15]

In short, the dogs helped to gather the individuals into the circle for prayer and the leader provided a prayerful focus. Beyond that, however, each individual 'prayed' in their own way—some participating, some sleeping, or some attempting to interact with the dogs. Each session during the study was an adventure. As dog ministry received enthusiastic reviews in the evaluations conducted at the end of the study, the sessions have become a part of the Maryville culture of prayer and service.

Lesson 4.4: Chance Encounters

As was mentioned earlier, perhaps the most frustrating thing for a study at Maryville was the 'open' campus environment. It became a challenge to visit those who were in the study because so many family members encountering the FFM teams on their way to a patient/resident's room made impromptu requests for the dogs to visit their loved ones, because "my mother/father/husband just loves dogs."

Added to these chance encounters, Pet Partners® protocols have set a two-hour-per-day limit for visitations. This makes the scheduling of individual visits and prayer-group gatherings a challenge. During the study, the FFMPC program coordinator took the information given to her by staff and, with her ministry partner, Barbara, attempted to visit the individuals who had requested visits as well as those in the study. Added to individual visitations was the challenge of fitting in a 20- to 30-minute prayer service during the two-hour window. Over the life of the study, it became evident that despite the number of impromptu requests, everyone who wanted a visit was able to receive one eventually.

As there are more and more requests, it will become more important for the FFMPC program coordinator, in conjunction with the ministry volunteers, to schedule visitation time carefully in order to cover the needs of those who have requested visits. There will always be those patients/residents who stop a FFM team in the hall, preventing them from going to a scheduled visit. However, having a brief discussion of who to visit before commencing visitation rounds or having a list of patients/residents to visit ensures that, at least, an attempt will be made to visit everyone on that list. As the program grows and expands, the importance of written visitation schedules will become more and more critical to ensure that everyone has a chance to interact with the dogs. In spiritual/pastoral care, the mantra is 'we deal'—meaning the Four-Footed Ministerial teams adjust to the situation, whatever it might be.

---

[15] One particular individual enjoyed clucking to the dogs to get them to come over. More often than not, both of the dogs would stay in the center of the gathering, sleeping. One individual who enjoyed being with the dogs was close enough to have her stocking foot on one of the dogs throughout one whole session. The dog, however, remained motionless the whole time. The resident was happy and so was the dog.

Checklist for Chaplains

❖ For an example of visitation elements that form the basis for training sessions for both volunteers and spiritual/pastoral-care providers, review Appendix E: Maryville FFMPC Program-Training Module Sample. This PowerPoint slide presentation/ script example provides a starting point for the development of in-house training sessions.

❖ Dog-ministry prayer-group gathering examples in Appendix C define the sequence of prayers and periods of silence for reflection. Various stories about animals can be used as a basis for the process of theological reflection. A column on the far right is included to record impressions of the session at its conclusion to enable the spiritual/ pastoral-care department to work on further refinements.

❖ Perhaps one of the biggest revelations that came from designing the program for Maryville was the importance of having Four-Footed Ministerial teams visit in pairs (See Unit Two, Discussion). The prescription for this comes from the New Testament where Jesus sent out His disciples two by two. Visiting in pairs proved to make tremendous sense (See Mark 6:7, NAB). Both the researcher and her ministry partner, Barbara, have been pleasantly surprised how this simple principle worked so well in the study and continues to enhance current interactions.

Bibliography

Banks, Marian R., and William A. Banks. "The Effects of Animal-Assisted Therapy on Loneliness in an Elderly Population in Long-Term Care Facilities." *Journal of Gerontology* 57A, no. 7 (2002): M428-M432.

Felton, Jerilyn E. "Four-Footed Ministers: A Roman Catholic Lay Pastoral Care Model for the Use of Canine Companions in Ministry to the Elderly in Retirement Communities." Marylhurst University, 2002.

_____. "'If I but Touch the Hem of His Cloak . . .': 'Touching Prayer' as the Best of Both Worlds." *Healing Ministry* 13, no. 3 (Summer, 2006): 7-9.

Giaquinto, Salvatore, and Fabio Valentini. "Is There a Scientific Basis for Pet Therapy?" *Disability and Rehabilitation* 31, no. 7 (2009): 595-598.

Gilbert, Rev. Richard B. "Chaplains and Charting." *Healing Ministry* 17, no. 3 (2011): 11-13.

Sweet, Leonard. *Nudge: Awakening Each Other to the God Who's Already There*. Colorado Springs, CO: David C. Cook, 2010.

Webb, Stephen H. "Pet Theories: A Theology for the Dogs." *Soundings* 78, no. 2, Summer (1995): 213-237.

THE CHAPLAIN/DIRECTOR'S ROLE IN IMPLEMENTATION

LESSON OVERVIEW:

This unit will discuss the chaplain/director's role in setting up, implementing, and maintaining the Four-Footed Ministers Pastoral-Care Program. This chapter presents helpful suggestions and resources.

LESSON OBJECTIVES:

❖ To learn more about the canine component of the program; learn how to sell the program to administration and infection control, working with helpful suggestions on how to stimulate relatively painless change within the organization; and finally, benefit from suggestions on recruiting and training.

❖ To continue to analyze and develop an in-house program based on the Four-Footed Ministers Pastoral-Care Program templates, moving forward toward implementation.

Lesson 5.1: Canine Companions 101

Before undertaking any big project, it is important to know something about the components that will be used. To that end, it is important that the chaplain/director know *something* about the "social lubricator" who makes the whole process of dog ministry work—the dog.

To quote a noted scholar in the field, "'it is scarcely possible to doubt that the love of man has become instinctive in the dog.' These words are taken from Charles Darwin's *The Origin of Species*, first published in 1859."[1] It is apparent to anyone watching dogs long enough or who has a dog as a companion pet that there is a bonding that takes place between the main caregiver and the dog. It becomes a process of developing a loving relationship where each gives of the self to the other in myriad ways. While what follows is not an extensive treatment of the canine companion, three canine behaviors will be examined because they relate directly to an effective dog-ministry program. These were chosen because they are often misunderstood and must be appreciated in order to grasp the importance of behavioral predictability, controllability, and reliability when working in ministry with an animal.[2]

What's With All That Sniffing?

Alexandra Horowitz studied animal behaviors and wrote about her work in her book, *Inside of a Dog: What Dogs See, Smell, and Know*. Published in 2009, this highly engaging book on dogs corrects many of the misunderstandings that humans have developed over the centuries relating to what this animal understands about the world around them, the nature of their interactions with other dogs, and their bonding with humans.

The dog picks up all sorts of scents from the surroundings that inform her about what is happening or has happened. The surroundings will tell a dog who has been by, what they had for breakfast, and if they are 'available.' Not only that, but Horowitz mentions that there is the aspect of time built into what a dog understands from sniffing, because "while we can see one of the petals [of a flower] drying and browning, the dog can smell this process of decay and aging."[3] Many of the smells that humans describe as pungent, a dog will find irresistible.

This fact points to the importance of a Four-Footed Minister responding quickly to a voice/hand signal to "leave it," because many patients/residents have often dropped food on their clothing or wheelchairs, forming a perfectly delectable two-week-old snack for a dog. This ensures that the animal is safe in case there is the possibility of something harmful on the floor or wheelchair such as an overlooked medication that was dropped or spilled.

---

[1] Jeffrey Moussaieff Masson, *Dogs Never Lie About Love* (New York: Three Rivers Press, 1997), xv. This important quotation begins his book that discusses this love between humans and dogs.

[2] The actual level of obedience training and specifications for the owner-handler in order to become a registered Pet Partners® team are covered in the *Pet Partners® Student Manual*. The work, *Animal-Assisted Therapy: Therapeutic Interventions*, provides additional directions on using dogs in a therapeutic environment. Chaplain/director should consult these books for the basics on registration with Pet Partners®.

[3] Alexandra Horowitz, *Inside of a Dog: What Dogs See, Smell and Know* (New York: Scribner, 2009), 72.

I Only Have Eyes for You

"Look at a dog in the eyes and you get the definite feeling that he is looking back. Dogs return our gaze," according to Horowitz.[4] This aspect of being able to connect visually is very important in spiritual/pastoral care. Connecting to another visually is where the spiritual/pastoral-care provider can read feelings beyond the words expressed, often intuiting a message the words did not communicate, but which is expressed in that person's eyes.[5]

Just as in human language, the dog language of gazing can have many meanings. It is a dog-behavior fact that an aggressive dog will use the power of gazing to express dominance and the dog recipient will avert that gaze to diffuse the uncomfortable situation.[6] While aggressive dogs cannot become Pet Partners®, the spiritual/pastoral-care provider should be aware of this behavior because the act of gazing in this instance can be an asset in ministry. In dog ministry, the practitioner will use this behavior, encouraging the dog to seek interaction with others through eye contact and thus, facilitating spiritual/pastoral-care interactions. Many patients/residents in the Maryville study commented on the beauty of the gaze that each of the dogs returned to those who sought to catch their eyes. Both were real charmers when it came to looking at those who sought to pet them.

Working like a Dog

In assessing interior states of being humans judge other humans and animals on what they observe from their behavior.[7] Dogs are no different. Horowitz states that dogs do sense their owner's anxiety in visitation situations and become anxious,[8] exhibiting stress-reducing behaviors such as licking their lips, yawning, shifting their weight, and panting. A well-trained FFM team works together during visitations and spiritual/pastoral-care interactions with the dog facilitating connection through its presence and the human being responsible for the dog's safety and well-being. Therefore, the FFM teams will often take short 'potty' breaks because the human counterpart has determined that the animal is feeling stressed, exhibiting those signs mentioned above. As time limitations are a part of working with dogs, it is important to have an FFMPC program coordinator who not only has the spiritual/pastoral-care training but also possesses a history of working with dogs. This person can put together schedules for teams that make sense given the inherent stress of visiting. This ensures happy teams, happy dogs, and happy patients/residents.

---

[4] Ibid., 139.

[5] See Friedman, "PaRDes," 63-64. Rabbi Friedman comments on an encounter with a woman who was language-challenged and how eye connection was an affirmation that she had been heard.

[6] Horowitz, *Inside of a Dog,* 149.

[7] Mary Midgley, *Animals and Why They Matter* (Athens, GA: University of Georgia Press, 1983), 130-131.

[8] Horowitz, *Inside of a Dog*, 239.

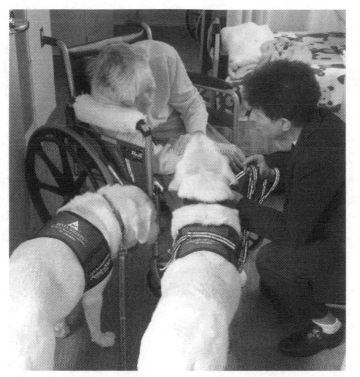

Caterina and Alya with Jerilyn and a study participant.

Lesson 5.2: Selling the Program
to Administration and Infection Control

One example of the recent research on the benefits of elder-animal interactions in healthcare facilities can be found in a pilot study conducted in an aged-care facility in Melbourne, Australia. Here, follow-up questionnaires confirmed that those elders who participated wanted the animals to continue to visit beyond the study. The researchers discovered that the participants had enjoyed the social interaction that occurred when the dogs visited. Moreover, study participants enjoyed the anticipation of future visits that provided a pleasing break to institutional life.[9] It follows that the benefits of instituting a preliminarily road-tested, safe, effective, and repeatable program for dog ministry formulated from the Maryville study far outweigh any burdens of implementing such a program. (See the discussion of the qualitative research study in Unit Two.)

Despite the many benefits, there are several objections to having a comprehensive program for ministry with dogs in healthcare facilities. The chaplain/director should be aware of these, should they surface in discussions about implementation of a dog-ministry program within their facility.

The first objection often raised is the argument that casual interactions with a dog handled by a spiritual/pastoral-care provider are effective and an in-house program is unnecessary. While this type of casual interaction does occur, there are no guarantees that

---

9   Lauren Prosser, Mardie Townsend, and Petra Staiger, "Older People's Relationships with Companion Animals: A Pilot Study," *Nursing Older People* 20, no. 3 (2008): 32.

an animal brought into the facility by a volunteer or chaplain is healthy and appropriately trained to interact with the patients/residents. Any dog lover knows that it is hard to evaluate one's own animal objectively and real behavioral problems can be overlooked. Moreover, if the animal has not been registered with a therapy organization, the facility could leave itself open for potential lawsuits if an accident occurs. An animal who is registered with Pet Partners® is one who should perform well and the owner/handler knows the protocols for safe interactions.

The second objection to a comprehensive program is that a resident dog would be much more effective in offering comfort on a continual basis. While this is true for general comfort and care, because of the nature of spiritual/pastoral-care interactions, the dog and volunteer or chaplain must act as a team and this is not possible if the animal has no special relationship with one person. In addition to this, though a resident dog appears as a good idea, the animal's care and comfort requires a staff member to be responsible for it. This could create staffing problems as well as jealousy between staff members.

The third objection that is often raised relates to studies that have demonstrated that virtual pets are a good substitute for live interactions.[10] While virtual pets can be helpful where actual live encounters are medically inadvisable, the Maryville qualitative study confirmed that virtual pets often isolate individuals, while the presence of live dogs was a magnet that drew patients/residents together. This noted enthusiastic response to dog visitations confirmed the general tendency of the scientific community to lean toward supporting live-animal visitation, provided appropriate safety protocols are in place.[11]

Another objection that might be raised to this program approach relates to the fact that the visitations and interactions were limited to dogs. While many different types of animals are registered by Pet Partners® for both therapy work and pet visitations, in the interest of conducting a manageable qualitative study on ministry with animals, the formulation of the Four-Footed Ministers Pastoral-Care Program was limited to dogs alone. The Maryville qualitative study confirmed that, while many residents had possessed cats in the past, they could still have fruitful interactions with the dog teams. Those invited into the study were not afraid of dogs, nor had they had a bad experience with them. A natural extension of the program to include other animals that Pet Partners® registers is a wide-open expanse for the curious researcher to explore.

Infection control is concerned, and rightly so, about animal-human cross-contamination. This objection, however, actually speaks the loudest in support of a comprehensive program rather than against it. The Four-Footed Ministers Pastoral-Care Program is based on Pet Partners® protocols that address these issues at length and provide guidance for volunteers and the chaplain/director. Therefore, while cross-contamination is always a possibility, with a comprehensive program in place, the risk is minimal.

---

[10]   Deborah L. Wells, "The Effect of Videotapes of Animals on Cardiovascular Responses to Stress," *Stress and Health* 21 (2005): 212-213, http://www.interscience.wiley.com, DOI: 10-1002/smi.1057 (accessed February 22, 2010).

[11]   Sarah J. Brodie, Francis C. Biley, and Michael Shewring, "An Exploration of the Potential Risks Associated with Using Pet Therapy in Healthcare Settings," *Journal of Clinical Nursing* 11 (2002): 446. A summary of ways to deal with zoonoses, diseases passed from animals to humans, to be found on 447 and 448.

Surprisingly, the biggest objection to dog ministry appears to originate from within the ranks of spiritual/pastoral care providers. One of the first objections raised by those in ministry is the question, "Can dogs really be ministers?" With the ever-increasing sensibility to the global chaos humans have caused, the issue of ministry as service can truly be defined in a wider context. Namely, if ministry *is* service to other humans, and the twenty-first-century person views all of creation as intimately connected, then the definition of ministry can and should be expanded to include the non-human, created as a gift for the human species.

While the six objections discussed above express legitimate concerns, each objection can be refuted. It can be surmised that administration will be favorably impressed with a Four-Footed Ministers Pastoral-Care Program because the program developed at Maryville was an *all-volunteer* program, having a minimal if any effect on the bottom line. Using Pet Partners®-registered dog teams relieved the facility of the burden of additional liability insurance purchase because Pet Partners®-registered dog teams are covered under a general liability-insurance policy when volunteering.[12]

Infection control should be satisfied that the use of Pet Partners® protocols, developed and implemented over many years of work in the field, would adequately balance the risk of ministry with dogs with the potential benefits of dog-human interactions that have been demonstrated in serious empirical studies.[13] While infection control often poses the most formidable obstacle to setting-up and implementing a Four-Footed Ministers Pastoral-Care Program, *The Pet Partners® Student Training Manual* devotes a whole section to this topic that is quite comprehensive.[14] This student manual provides a step-by-step introduction on safety issues for the Pet Partners®-registered team. This manual also provides a "Sample Infection Control Policy" that can be molded to fit the healthcare facility's needs.[15] Finally, infection control can receive additional information at the CDC website at

http://www.cdc.gov/healthypets/pdf/petscript_general.pdf

The document at this web address describes a 'pet-scription' that can be signed by a health professional and is a good guide for nursing-care staff. Further, it confirms the importance of the protocols that Pet Partners® has already set up to ensure safe interactions between humans and animals.

Though there is a charge for facility registration with Pet Partners®, startup costs in the Maryville study were minimal. This registration entitled the facility to be listed on Pet Partners® website (www.petpartners.org) and the local representative was alerted to the

---

[12]   It is suggested that any recruitment or training materials might include a disclaimer outlining the specific levels of liability coverage provided by Pet Partners® and the facility. Pet Partners® carries a general liability-insurance policy on volunteers in the amount of $2,000,000. Each facility can specify the level of their commitment in this area to ease volunteers' concerns about liability coverage.

[13]   Brodie, Biley, and Shewring, 445.

[14]   Julie Miller and Katherine Connor, "Going to the Dogs . . . For Help," *Nursing 2000* 30, no. 11 (2000). See pages 65-67 of this article, which provide a good summary of the benefits of dog visitation as well as a summary of Pet Partners® protocols.

[15]   Delta Society, *Pet Partners® Team Training Course Manual* (Bellvue, WA: Delta Society, 2008). See pages 6-12 through 6-18.

need for dog teams to participate in the qualitative study. Moreover, the researcher was able to secure a modest grant from the Sisters of the Holy Names of Jesus and Mary that covered many of the incidental costs. Therefore, there was no significant financial impact on the operating budget of Maryville.

As the Four-Footed Ministers Pastoral-Care Program was built on solid time-tested Pet Partners® protocols, many of the questions as to formulation of a procedure for the program have already been addressed in the Four-Footed Ministers Pastoral-Care Program Protocols (See Appendix D). If there are any questions with regard to the spiritual/pastoral-care component, these could be researched by the FFMPC program coordinator who, in conjunction with the chaplain/director, is responsible for incorporating changes to the program into the volunteer training manual. Therefore, the study provided a solid though preliminary foundation for the integration of the program into the Maryville facility.

If additional assistance is needed, the chaplain/director can visit Pet Partners® website or call the headquarters for more information and direction to other resources that will help support the case for the inclusion of the Four-Footed Ministers Pastoral-Care Program into the spiritual/pastoral care department.

Chaplain's/Director's Tool Kit for Helping to Create Change

When an organization considers something new, fear of change is one of the first emotions that surfaces. It is a fact of human nature that changes in procedures within an organization will create stress and anxiety. Therefore, if a chaplain/director can be armed with tools to help create a climate where change happens as painlessly and naturally as possible, it is more likely that staff and patients/residents will perceive the beneficial aspects of the changes and be able to adjust relatively easily to any negative ones that might come to light.

In order to provide a structure for change to take place easily, Chip and Dan Heath, in their book *Switch: How to Change Things When Change is Hard*, began with a story based on a simple example taken from a work by Jonathan Haidt, *The Happiness Hypothesis*.[16] Building on Haidt's image of an elephant guided by a rider where the elephant is the emotional side of an individual and the rider is the rational one, the brothers use this image to construct three simple directives that could assist others in appreciating the process of change: direct the rider, motivate the elephant, and shape the path.[17]

In directing the rider, the brothers mention three actions that help to focus on the change that will happen within the organization. The first is selecting a story that will tell more about how beneficial the proposed program will be when instituted. For example, in speaking with administration, the chaplain can tell the stories that have come their way in reference to the intense love that patients/residents express when talking about the comfort and care their own pets have provided. Secondly, the chaplain can discuss with staff how having an FFM team visit will boost the spirits of their charges, creating a pleasant atmosphere. Finally, when explaining the Four-Footed Ministers Pastoral-Care Program, the chaplain can remind

---

[16] Chip Heath and Dan Heath, *Switch: How to Change Things when Change is Hard* (New York: Broadway Books, 2010), 7.

[17] Ibid., 259.

the staff of how their mission statement can be achieved with the help of the FFM teams who visit on a regular basis.

In order to control the emotional aspect of the human person, characterized by an unruly and possibly overpowering elephant, the brothers suggest "motivating the elephant." Realizing that the elephant is the emotional side of the human person and is strongly driven by desire, the chaplain should illustrate how the FFM team can create a climate of calm and care by using a concrete example, e.g., having a FFM team visit with the administrator and senior-level staff in one of their meetings. Prior to undertaking this, it is important to check with administration and staff to ensure that no one is allergic to dogs nor has any fear of them. At this same meeting, the chaplain can suggest that the FFM team that they have met could visit on a temporary basis for a short period of time, being able to revisit the issue of the inclusion of a full-blown program after a period of probation. This focus, "shrinking the change," makes the proposed addition of the program manageable.[18] The final suggestion the brothers make in the section discussing "motivat[ing] the elephant" is "growing your people."[19] Here, the chaplain can ask for volunteers from the ranks of the senior-staff level and below who have dogs and would like to serve with them as probationary volunteers. This might present these volunteers with scheduling challenges because of the limitations specified in Pet Partners® protocols, but these can be managed effectively.[20] Moreover, local Pet Partners® representatives may be available to conduct classes for interested staff and evaluate the potential FFM team for Pet Partners® registration, making the possibility of an in-house program more likely.

The final directive the Heath brothers present is to "shape the path."[21] Here is the opportunity for the chaplain to be truly collaborative with those staff interested in volunteering for the Four-Footed Ministers Pastoral-Care Program development. Those staff members who would relish the chance to share their canine companion in a spiritual/pastoral way can be encouraged to work with the chaplain to develop a pilot program for their own organization. People who have input in designing the change will be more likely to come on board with that change. Effective change will require the staff who volunteer to build the habit of "scheduling in" their visitation times because their work as a FFM team must be volunteer in nature.[22] Finally, "rally the herd" is the final suggestion for "shaping the path."[23] If the chaplain is behind the development of the facility's own Four-Footed Ministers Pastoral-Care Program and is excited about the possibilities, the staff will catch the enthusiasm generated. As enthusiasm creates an atmosphere of adventure, those staff members who want to become a part of the organization's mission beyond their own professional efforts can help to change the facility's procedures to encompass their own, in-house program for dog ministry. These

---

[18]   Ibid.

[19]   Ibid.

[20]   Dogs must be Pet Partners®-registered when working as a Four-Footed Ministerial team. In addition, there is a two-hour per day limit on dog visitation, according to the Four-Footed Ministers Pastoral-Care Program and Pet Partners® protocols.

[21]   Ibid.

[22]   See extensive discussion of liability issues in *Pet Partners® Student Training Manual*, page 6.12 through page 6.18.

[23]   Heath and Heath, *Switch*, 259.

simple suggestions can help the chaplain with ways they might work with administration and staff to create a comprehensive dog-ministry program.

Lesson 5.3: Recruiting and Training Volunteers: Volunteers or Spiritual-Care Providers

As the Four-Footed Ministers Pastoral-Care Program is currently an all-volunteer program, contacting Pet Partners® Headquarters (www.petpartners.org) to discover if there is a local representative is the next step. A Pet Partners® representative may be able direct the chaplain/director to individuals who might be interested in the program and possibly could fill the job of FFMPC program coordinator.

Though this program is new, the interest in dog ministry is ever increasing. One good place for recruiting an FFMPC program coordinator is a university or seminary in the area. With the culture becoming more aware of the uses of dogs in various helping fields, those in seminary may be eager to discover new possibilities for ministry with a holistic focus. The Four-Footed Ministers Pastoral-Care Program fits in well within this focus.

Beginning with one's own faith community, the chaplain/director can canvas fellow parish/congregation members for those who might be interested in using their dogs in ministry. Many individuals might already be or might be interested in becoming Pet Partners®.

In order to ensure that volunteers are comfortable with the roles they will play in dog ministry, there are *two* job descriptions provided, as was discussed in Lesson 3.2. Those who wish to participate but choose not to pursue additional spiritual-care training will function as advocates for their dogs, similar to the role of a volunteer in animal-assisted therapy. The direction of spiritual/pastoral-care interactions is the responsibility of the chaplain/director or FFMPC program coordinator and not the volunteer. This alleviates the fear that many individuals may feel at being asked to be a part of a ministerial endeavor.[24]

The job description designated as "spiritual-care provider" can be filled by an individual a background in spiritual/pastoral care, such as a chaplain or one who has had experience in Clinical Pastoral Education (CPE), or holds a graduate Certificate of Pastoral Care. If the chaplain/director wishes to participate in the program with their own dog, there are issues of facility liability that should be addressed by administration. Currently, the Pet Partners® general liability-insurance policy would *not cover* chaplains during their spiritual/pastoral-care interactions with their animal. This issue of professional liability coverage for a FFM team is one that will need to be addressed at some later date.

In Appendix B, there is an example of two training-session outlines where the chaplain/director and FFMPC program coordinator work in tandem to explain the volunteer procedures of the facility as well as those aspects that relate specifically to the Four-Footed Ministers

---

[24] The researcher experienced one instance where an invitation was extended to a potential Pet Partners®-registered volunteer dog team, but was refused. The individual was spiritual-but-not-religious, assuming that the job required one to be of a particular faith. Moreover, the researcher has also encountered resistance about the issue of spiritual/pastoral care from within Pet Partners® ranks.

Pastoral-Care Program.[25] A separate PowerPoint presentation on the program provides the volunteers with a look at how the program works within the facility.[26] At these training sessions, both one-on-one and dog-ministry prayer-group gatherings should be explained to and explored with the volunteers. Appropriate forms should also be discussed and reporting procedures reviewed.

The training sessions were designed to orient a group of both "volunteer" and spiritual-care providers to the basics of dog ministry. Based on the number of volunteers, these training sessions were designed to cover approximately a four-hour period, two hours for each segment. Additional training for the spiritual-care providers could be scheduled after this initial session, as their commitment is more extensive. Follow-up training should occur as needed so that the highest level of care is offered and maintained.

**A study participant with Caterina and Barbara on the left
and Alya and Jerilyn on the right.**

---

[25] Part of the duties of the chaplain at Maryville is the orientation of volunteers and thus, in this instance, there is no additional cost to the facility for this training.

[26] See Appendix E: for the copy of the Maryville training presentations.

Lesson 5.4: Training Staff

If the chaplain/director has done their preliminary work well, training staff on what to expect when the dogs come into the facility should be an easy task.[27] An explanation of the history of the program[28] and its function should help staff to see that having the dogs assist in good spiritual/pastoral care will make their jobs much easier. Patients/residents will have the opportunity to experience the joy of 'having,' if only for a brief moment, a dog to pet and with whom to interact. These interactions will create an environment that results in happier patients/residents and happier staff.

From the Maryville study, it became evident that there was a very important component that had been overlooked in the initial setup of the orientation presentation. In that initial presentation, there was no appreciation for the diverse mix of countries represented by the CNAs as well as the nursing staff. Many of the CNAs came from cultures that might have a problem understanding the American sensibility that views dogs as full members of the family. In some Asian cultures, for example, there could be some confusion as to why a person would want to interact with a dog, because dogs are gastronomical delights. To address this oversight, one slide in the presentation (Appendix E) gives an explanation of the American culture's love of canines and that many of the patients/residents would enjoy interacting with dogs on a regular basis.

Lesson 5.5: You are Not Alone—Local Resources

As was mentioned previously, you as chaplain/director are not alone. The first connection you should make is with the staff at Pet Partners®, as they are willing and able to help you locate those individuals in your area who can be valuable resources for you. They can provide information on and referrals to resources such as the local Humane Society or dog trainers in the area who might have students interested in dog ministry. It is these connections made online and in person that will enable your program to become known in the area, thereby encouraging other faith communities to join your efforts to bring a comprehensive dog-ministry program to the patients/residents within your facility. With the aid of dedicated volunteers and the resources to be found at local universities and seminaries, your program will develop over time. As more and more of those working in ministry get involved in the Four-Footed Ministers Pastoral-Care Program, the result can be greater assistance for you, the chaplain/director, in honing and perfecting the procedures of your facility that will raise the level of spiritual/pastoral care offered. In the end, everybody wins.

---

[27] See Appendix E.

[28] See Unit One, Lesson 1.2 for more information for presentation information. Print templates for training session design are available in Appendix E.

Checklist for Chaplains

❖ Contact Pet Partners® at www.petpartners.org for the name of the local Pet Partners® representative.

❖ For additional reading, see Appendix B: Program Forms, Exhibit D: Resources for Animal-Assisted Interventions and CAM/PS.

❖ To sell the program to administration/infection control remember that:

  ○ **The program is road-tested**. The Four-Footed Ministers Pastoral-Care Program was built on a nine-month qualitative study conducted at Maryville Nursing Home in Beaverton, Oregon and Pet Partners® protocols.

  ○ **The program is safe.** In building upon time-tested protocols developed by Pet Partners®, modified and adjusted based on ongoing research in the field, safe interactions are of the highest priority. The Four-Footed Ministers Pastoral-Care Program recruits only currently registered Pet Partners® teams and follows the Pet Partners® protocols.

  ○ **The program is effective.** The results of the Maryville study, though preliminary, confirmed the value of the program for the study participants who voiced their unanimous approval of the program with only minor enhancements suggested. Residents at Maryville requested that the program continue and it is currently ongoing.

  ○ **The program is repeatable.** Because both Pet Partners® and the Four-Footed Ministers Pastoral-Care Program have defined a structure for the operation, if the chaplain/director or the FFMPC program coordinator should move on, the program can continue. Moreover, as this is a program that is developed within the facility, program modifications can be made as required and the written records kept for future review and enhancement.

❖ Contact local universities and seminaries as well as other faith communities in the area for potential candidates for the FFMPC program coordinator's position or potential volunteers. Work with universities or seminaries to develop synergistic relationships where seminary students could function as intern chaplains with their Pet Partners®-registered dogs.

❖ Training staff, "volunteers," and spiritual-care providers can be accomplished through two lesson plans (See Appendix B, Program Forms, Exhibit G) and a short PowerPoint slide show (See Appendix E: Maryville FFMCP Program-Training Module Sample).

❖ To the question, "Can we set up a Four-Footed Ministers Pastoral-Care Program?" the answer should be a resounding "Yes, we can!" Enjoy interacting and developing an in-house program for dog ministry, knowing that you are improving the lives of the residents, their families, and the staff in your facility.

Bibliography

Brodie, Sarah J., Francis C. Biley, and Michael Shewring. "An Exploration of the Potential Risks Associated with Using Pet Therapy in Healthcare Settings." *Journal of Clinical Nursing*, no. 11 (2002): 444-456.

Delta Society. *Pet Partners® Team Training Course Manual*. Bellevue, WA: Delta Society, 2008.

Friedman, Rabbi Dayle A. "PaRDeS: A Model for Presence in *Hitlavut Ruchanit*." In *Jewish Pastoral Care: A Practical Handbook from Traditional and Contemporary Sources*. Woodstock, VT: Jewish Lights Publishing, 2001. 60-73.

Heath, Chip, and Dan Heath. *Switch: How to Change Things When Change Is Hard*. New York: Broadway Books, 2010.

Horowitz, Alexandra. *Inside of a Dog: What Dogs See, Smell and Know*. New York: Scribner, 2009.

Masson, Jeffrey Moussaieff. *Dogs Never Lie About Love*. New York: Three Rivers Press, 1997.

Midgley, Mary. *Animals and Why They Matter*. Athens, GA: University of Georgia Press, 1983.

Miller, Julie, and Katherine Connor. "Going to the Dogs . . . For Help." *Nursing 2000* 30, no. 11 (2000): 65-67.

Prosser, Lauren, Mardie Townsend, and Petra Staiger. "Older People's Relationships with Companion Animals: A Pilot Study." *Nursing Older People* 20, no. 3 (2008): 29-32.

Wells, Deborah L. "The Effect of Videotapes of Animals on Cardiovascular Responses to Stress." *Stress and Health* 21 (2005). http://www.interscience.wiley.com. DOI: 10.1002/ smi.1057 (accessed February 22, 2010).

APPENDICES

APPENDIX A:

RESEARCH NOTES

Exhibit A: Notes on General Visitations Important Study Entries

Note Date: September 3, 2010

As soon as we entered the facility, we began to encounter residents who wanted to interact with both Caterina and Alya. As we walked around, we interacted with residents who wanted to know more about the dogs. Barbara shared their story with those who asked. It was a great opportunity for residents and their family members to interact with the dogs. We had opportunities to interact with staff as well. As our intention was to introduce the dogs to those in the study, we made it a point to call on the study participants to introduce them to Barbara and Caterina. They made a big hit with those in the study who were available in their rooms. Some declined a visit because of ill health, but generally the dogs were well received and both dogs reacted positively to the interactions.

Observations:

1. Following Jesus' directive in sending disciples out in pairs, we discovered that, when doing canine-assisted ministry/pastoral and spiritual care, it is good to go in pairs. It is a great way to train future FFM teams.
2. We will have a challenge in separating the study participants from other residents. I will have to keep good notes as I encounter our study participants, as many who are not in the study want to share their experiences of their dogs with us.
3. Barbara commented on the value of the ecumenical focus of our efforts, as we come from two different streams of Christianity (Presbyterian and Roman Catholic).

Note Date: September 17, 2010

There were several things that came out of our visits:

1. Sister will meet with us after our rounds to debrief. The information she gives us is valuable for understanding each of the study participants.
2. I notice how we are interacting with more and more people in the "meet-and-greet" mode. This is part of our work and in this area we do not get into any personal issues. It will provide me with opportunities to contrast "meet and greet" with spiritual care because our visits in those instances (meet and greet) are superficial.
3. It seems as if our visitations are expanding to a wider clientele just because of our visibility.
4. Barbara suggested we ask how the visits are being received. Perhaps this is a good follow-up for me.

Note Date: September 24, 2010

Observations from visits:

1. We have a "built in" quasi-control group in that residents and the people who visit them are free to interact with the dogs as soon as we enter the facility. This happens quite frequently. Sometimes we are unable to begin our visits until everyone in the area has interacted with the dogs.
2. We often have people who were not in the study make comments and share stories about their animals. Though these specific stories cannot be used in the study, it does illustrate the point that the dogs provide a gathering point for safe interactions; the dogs fulfill their role as social lubricators. Visitors, staff, and residents come to interact with them and seem to enjoy the interaction with Barbara or me much more than if we were just a friendly stranger/volunteer without a dog.
3. One individual NOT in the study is Joseph.[1] Joseph is a very mentally sharp resident in a motorized wheelchair who goes out of his way to interact with the dogs. He was particularly attentive to Alya today and likes to pet her, but even more importantly, he liked just look at her. One of the staff social workers was on his way down the hall and stopped to pet Alya. Again, the conversation was lively and engaging for the subject matter was the love of dogs. Everyone, myself included, felt better after that interchange.

Note Date: October 1, 2010

Observations:

1. Barbara and I had a chance to sit down and process our various visits. Barbara said that the dogs were "a bridge" that made visitation very easy. We keep experiencing over and over how the dogs permit us admission to a person's life through physical interaction and help us create community.
2. Sister seemed to be very busy with new residents coming in and flowers delivered. We had wanted to debrief with her, but she must have not heard the page. I will touch base with her about adding two new participants, Joseph and R., to our list of visits, as these two people are becoming regulars in our visitation schedule.

Note Date: October 8, 2010

We had various people stop us to ask about the dogs. We began by visiting R., who is not a member of the study because she is not a long-term-care resident. She does love to see the dogs. We tried to ask her more about her own connection to dogs. We covered much of the same ground we had in previous visits. We did have a chance to contact study participants who had not attended the outing to the "Pumpkin Patch."

---

[1] The names of the study participants are fictitious to protect their identities. Initials are used to indicate those who interacted with the Four-Footed Ministerial teams but were not part of the study. Joseph did join the study after September 24, 2010.

Observations:

1. As mentioned, those who are not in the study have formed a quasi-control group. People are curious about the dogs. We field the same questions over and over but are pleased to inform the inquirers about the dog-ministry study.
2. We have a new participant, Joseph. I had asked him if he would be willing to learn more about the study and participate. He agreed. Sister had confirmed that he would be a good participant and could sign an informed consent on his own recognizance.
3. Alya did not want to go into Dinah's room. She had that reaction when visiting my late husband before he died. Caterina also picked up on Alya's reaction and became reticent to stay in the room. Given the bad news that Dinah received from her doctor, the dogs might have sensed a change in her condition. Both Barbara and I have offered to be with her as she transitions. If the dogs can be there and if staff will permit it, perhaps they will be able to help.

We visited for about 1 ½ hrs. That seemed to be the maximum the dogs could tolerate today.

Note Date: November 5, 2010

We had an hour to process with Sister today and we will begin our Thursday rather than Friday visitations this month rather than next month.

We discovered that Seth's sister Jael is in the room across the hall from him and I will email Sister an informed consent form for her because she really enjoyed talking with Barbara and petting Caterina. Caterina was a bit quieter than normal today, but was willing to engage with those who wanted to pet her. Jael was very excited about petting the dogs.

We continue to have difficulty getting around the building because so many people want to visit with the dogs. We even had a new resident, F., who came in yesterday, want to interact with the dogs. Her son M. saw us walking down the hall and asked us to come in. Barbara and I had a wonderful, welcoming visit with F. and will stop in to see her next week. It appears that we seem to have as many people who are "in" the study interacting with the dogs as those who are not part of the formal qualitative study.

It appears as if both Caterina and Alya had great visits because they did not exhibit many signs of stress. I was much more careful to make sure that Alya and Caterina had breaks outside for potty time and for a relief from visitation. Further, Barbara also mentioned that pairing up, following the biblical model of Jesus, has been working very, very well. I will make sure that it becomes a part of the program.

One of the good effects of dog ministry for Maryville is the fact that the facility received a donation based on the fact that there were dogs in the facility. That says something about the creation of a homey atmosphere where the residents are happy and engaged.

We will meet on Thursday and have a short pet-grief support gathering at 11:30 for those who have already expressed interest in this service. I have two women who have contacted me about it. We also have a staff member who will attend. We can see if this particular service will be an ongoing one or if it will be held on an as-needed basis. [*Due to a waning interest in pet-grief support gatherings, this part of the study was not pursued in depth. See*

"Notes on Pet Grief Support Gatherings at Maryville" following these "Notes on General Visitations."]

Note Date: November 11, 2010

We discovered that the gathering spot has become the beauty shop where we meet many of the residents. We unofficially call on one woman who is somewhat withdrawn but has really enjoyed interacting with the dogs and we call on her every week, just to say hello. Her eyes light up when she sees the dogs.

A new resident whom we met the previous week loves to see the dogs and we came by her room, but she was not there. We saw her later outside of the beauty shop where she was going in to have her hair done. Though in compromised health, she also enjoyed petting the dogs.

Another woman we happened upon is a woman who has difficulty speaking. However, she does make herself understood, especially where the dogs are concerned. Again, the dogs make her day.

Today we were asked by a staff to visit a resident who really missed his dog. We did call on him and he was so happy to see us. He will be another person we will put on our list to visit. [This resident died suddenly after the study concluded.]

I will propose that we try to visit our "study participants" first then make the rounds to those who are not in the study. We are limited by a two-hour window, which is the maximum time that the dogs should visit as Pet Partners®-registered therapy dogs. We will have to triage our visits. Because of the success of our efforts in dog-ministry visitation, the only other course of action appears be to suspend the study and make only general observations of our interactions. I feel this is a bit premature at this point, but I will suggest this in an email.

Note Date: December 2, 2010

I will increase my visitation times during the month of December to re-establish connections that may have grown fuzzy during our absence in November.

We have seen some remarkable interactions with individuals who have encountered the teams:

1. There is one woman D. who seems to have dementia and is physically challenged who likes interacting with the dogs. Her private care giver helped D. to interact with Alya. Alya connected to D. through licking her hand and this is the way this woman can communicate, for she can no longer talk nor move at will. It is through TOUCH that she can communicate with Alya and with others.
2. We were able to interact with a woman because Alya licked her hand in greeting. This woman can only make unintelligible sounds but can use her good hand to pet Alya and express her joy touching her. The woman makes the same sound over and over, often very loudly, but we know that she is delighted to interact with the dogs because of the tenor of the sound she makes.

3. We called on V., whose dog had died. His connection to dogs is strong for he had a comforter with pictures of dogs on it. He was very much "with it" today and thanked us for coming.
4. We were asked to call on B., who had been moved into the Alzheimer's unit. Her son saw the dogs in the hall and asked that we visit her because she is a new resident in the unit and needed help getting acclimated.
5. We had the chance to meet those residents of the Alzheimer's unit who were in a physical exercise class conducted in the open space. The facilitator was glad to see us and we will attempt to add this unit on our rounds.

The dogs seem to be doing their magic in connecting people because they always draw a crowd when they show up. Moreover, one factor against the use of virtual pets is the fact that real dogs create a community whereas virtual pets are objects that one person possesses and does not necessarily draw others to it. This is an important observation that was confirmed by Barbara stating that the "theology of touch" is so very important to elders who are often "handled" rather than lovingly touched. As ministers, we can hope to touch others through our presence; dogs do this naturally.

Additional visit—December 5, 2010 (Jerilyn and Alya)

Generally, Sundays are quiet without the hubbub of the week. Unless there is an activity, this seems to be a good time to really "visit" with our study participants. We can have extended spiritually focused visits.

Abigail made a suggestion for the "group prayer-service." So that Dinah (in hospice) could attend, she suggested that we hold our gathering on the unit in the dining room. We had originally planned our gathering for Thursdays at 11:30 and this might not be a good time. Our next option would be to hold the gathering in Dinah's room, but due to the number of attendees, that may not work either. I can read Dinah the story for reflection in her room after we have the dog-ministry prayer-group gathering. On the other hand, we might use the gathering as an incentive for Dinah to come out of her room. It might help her to interact with others.

Note Date: December 16, 2010

I have noticed that there seem to be a core group of people with whom we can connect on a regular basis: Sarah, Dinah, and Sean. I think this is due to the fact that they value the visits of the dogs. In fact, Sarah has "dogs" written in on her calendar.

I was very surprised to notice that when we entered the facility, the administrator was behind the desk in reception. She said that she wanted to get in touch with what happens in this most public area of the whole facility. As we were leaving, she commented to us how much the dogs meant to the residents and she thanked us for our efforts. That comment was greatly appreciated.

Additional Visitation Day: Sunday, December 19, 2010

General Observations: Judith, R., and Joseph, three people who love dogs, expressed their connection to Alya both verbally as well as through petting her. They mentioned the fact that we all had a very easy time connecting. Because she is a beautiful dog, the poster child for the Four-Footed Ministers Pastoral-Care Program, she is easy to approach. This confirms once again the importance of having a dog to help lead us into a 'spiritual' space where it might be difficult to enter. Dog leadership in this area became most powerfully evident when we visited Dinah, who is in the process of transitioning. She loved dogs and we can reestablish a connection very quickly because of Alya's presence. This is an area for further exploration as we move forward in time.

Additional Visitation Sunday: December 26, 2010

Generally it was very quiet in the facility on this day after Christmas. Those who were present were in their rooms or in the dining room playing Bingo.
Observations:

1. Dinah might be getting closer to the end of her journey as she talks about moving. I don't know if this is her way of processing her death preparation or if it reflects her actual course of action. She stated that her doctor has found her a foster-care home AND had secured a dog for her, a miniature greyhound that can be hers in the new facility.
2. Sean is doing very well, but we need to give him more time to express himself. I am not sure that he will be teaching a class because of his general health, but time will tell.
3. Abigail was very chatty and is a woman who constantly speaks highly about others, re-directing the conversation to others' needs. She is a joy to be around.

Note Date: December 30, 2010

The general mood in the facility was one of celebration. There is going to be a New Year's Eve party that is scheduled for December 31, 2010 at 1:30 p.m. Many of the residents were very excited to be able to attend. The participants in the study had also picked up the excitement that permeated the facility.
Observations:

1. Alya definitely is a 'social lubricator' for our visits. Unless the person does not like dogs (we did run into one lady in the hall that said she did not want to interact with Alya), everyone flocks to pet her. This is the way to begin connecting to people.
2. A non-participant who must have had a very severe stroke (she cannot speak or move) is very happy to see Alya. She appears to cry when she is able to pet her. I understand from her caregiver that she loves dogs. Her caregiver has to position her hand so that she can interact with Alya, but the effect is truly amazing. She appears to come alive with happiness.

Note Date: January 6, 2011

We had a short debriefing session with Sister Josephine. We went over the various residents we had visited. This time is very important for us as we only visit once a week and need to know more about the spiritual state of those whom we visit.
Observations:

1. We had asked to get onto the January "Calendar of Events" but saw that we were not listed for the January 13th or January 27th dates. Sister said she would make sure that we get on the January 27th schedule.
2. We will draw on the power of music for our first dog-ministry prayer-group gathering. We will ask a member of the group (Sean) to lead us in the final blessing.
3. We have determined that it is important to have debriefing sessions with the chaplain after visits. It is in these sessions that we truly act as both an advocate for the program and the residents, for it is here we receive important updates as to any special conditions of the residents who might want visits.

Note Date: January 20, 2011

Several things happened during our visits today that have bearing on the development of the program. One of those developments points to what dog-ministry's goal should be through the theology of touch.
Observations:

1. With many residents I find that visitation with the dogs brightens their day. The visits seem to lift the boredom of being in the same location day-in and day-out. As we are still within the parameters of the study and I can see the benefit the dog visits are having on the wider population, I believe that there will be more work to be done after the study is completed because of the challenges we face with both physical and mental concerns of the long-term resident population.
2. We interacted with a resident, D., whose private caregiver came searching for us. D. has many physical challenges, but her face lit up the room when she saw us in a meeting with Sister Josephine. Sister snapped a couple of pictures of Alya with D. Barbara noticed how Sister seemed pleasantly surprised at D.'s reaction to seeing the dogs. D., who probably has a diminished sense of touch as well as her apparent physical challenges, made grateful sounds as her caregiver guided her hand to pet Alya, who connected with her by licking her hand. Alya particularly liked interacting with both C., the caregiver, and with D.; she was wagging her tail and had her ears up. Both reactions speak volumes when looking at the 'theology of touch'.

Note Date: February 27, 2011

I visited on February 27, a Sunday, to let the residents in the study know that I would be gone the following week and the week after that. I was able visit with Sean. It is such a joy to see him. He was glad to see Alya and me. We visited with him for a short while and he gave Alya and me his blessing as we left.

I called on one other resident, Jael. She was sitting alone in her room and was so glad to see us. She even asked if it was Alya or Caterina that was visiting. She is a wonderful person to visit. She was so grateful that we came to see her. I will have to check in with Sister to see how things are going with her family.

These notes were selected because they illustrate the observations that helped the researcher to structure the Four-Footed Ministers Pastoral-Care Program. For the complete discussion of the qualitative study, see Unit Two.

Exhibit B: Notes on Pet Grief Support Gatherings at Maryville Date: Began September 9, 2010

Note Date: September 9, 2010

No one came to this first gathering that was advertised on the web newsletter. I emailed Lisa Zeiner, Pet Partners® program coordinator, about this. I suggested that we will hold our second gathering on a Saturday (October 16th) instead of on the previous Thursday, hoping for increased attendance. We had scheduled gatherings based on a need for a spiritually focused pet-grief support-group, a need that was originally expressed by Lisa.

Note Date: November 5, 2010

No one came to the second gathering. We decided to do pet-grief support by personal invitation. We determined that if Lisa Zeiner does receive inquiries for pet-grief support, she will email me and I will send a personal invitation to that individual who can meet with me privately or join others who wish to make a group. The issue of pet-grief support in a spiritual context is a moving target at this time. We will see where it goes from here and if we get any additional response from the two women who have already contacted me. We have one staff member who will come to meet with us. Again, we hope that will be a valuable service for those suffering from the loss of their pets.

Note Date: November 11, 2010

We had one woman come to our November 11th gathering. We decided to schedule our pet-grief support sessions once a month. Our next meeting will be December 9th at 11:30 a.m.

Note Date: December 9, 2010

No one came to this gathering. I did not have the chance to advertise it, so that could be one of the reasons for no one attending. *The Pet-Grief Support project will put on hold as we will be conducting dog-ministry prayer-group gatherings beginning in January 2011.*

Though no one came to the gathering, I did have the chance to process with one of the staff,[2] who talked about Buddy, her lab who had died the year before. Cathy said she had a picture of their four family Labrador Retrievers and would email it to me for inclusion in the training manual. I was very pleased that she shared her story with me about her beloved pet, who is buried at her parents' home along with the other family pets who have passed away. She mentioned that she visits their graves when she calls on the family.

She shared a story about a video taken this year where the family labs had been dressed in costumes for the season. She related how funny it was when they tried to run to catch a ball that had been flung into the air but were somewhat hampered by their costumes. Sharing her story seemed to be healing for her and she appreciated the 20 minutes we had

---

[2]   Permission was obtained from both Mr. Perrizo and Ms. Edwards to use their real names.

set aside so that she could tell her to tell her story of her beloved lab, Buddy and other family dogs.

Note Date: December 30, 2010

I saw Cathy and let her know I had received the picture of her dad with the labs eagerly waiting for dinner. This is a perfect picture that reflects Luther's comment about attentiveness in prayer that Christians should exhibit. The Christian in prayer should be like a dog waiting for a piece of meat: totally focused on the object of their desire. (Luther learned the lesson on attentiveness from his dog, Toelpel. See Richard Bainton, "Luther on Birds, Dogs and Babies: Gleanings from the 'Table Talk'" in *Luther Today*, edited by Roland H. Bainton, Warren A. Quanbeck, and E. Gordon Rupp, published by Luther College Press, 1957.)

**Photo: Mr. Jay Perrizo and
Buddy, Sandy (Hazelnut's
Puppy), Hazelnut, and
Boomer
Compliments of
Ms. Cathy Edwards,
Maryville Nursing Home**

Exhibit C: Final Interview Assessment—Sample Evaluation

Subjects: Sarah, Jael, Seth, Judith, Sean, Abigail, Joseph
Date: May 5, 2011

Resident:_____

Thank you for participating in the nine-month study on dog ministry. In order to assess how we might continue the program, we need your input on the effectiveness of our spiritual/ pastoral-care efforts.

One-On-One Visits:

1. What did you like or not like about being visited weekly by the dogs?
2. What can make these interactions better for you?

Dog-Ministry Prayer-Group Gatherings:

1. What did you like or not like about gathering as a group to hear scriptural readings related to an imaginative tale of Jesus and his pet dog?
2. What can we do to improve this experience for you?

Finally, tell us why or why not dog ministry made a difference in your relationship to God?

Exhibit D: RESOURCES FOR Animal-Assisted Interventions and CAM/PS

Below are general resources for Animal-Assisted Interventions and CAM/PS. Pet Partners® books can be ordered online from Pet Partners®. The work published by VDM Publishing can be ordered at Amazon.com.

Books

Bustad, Leo K. *Animals, Aging, and the Aged.* Minneapolis, MN: University of Minnesota, 1980.

Coren, Stanley. *How to Speak Dog.* New York: Free Press, a division of Simon and Schuster, 2003.

Cusack, Odean and Elaine Smith. *Pets and the Elderly: The Therapeutic Bond.* New York: Haworth Press, 1984.

Delta Society. *The Pet Partners® Team Training Course.* Renton, WA: Delta Society, 2008.

Delta Society. *Standards of Practice.* Renton, WA: Delta Society, 1996.

Felton, Jerilyn E. "Four-Footed Ministers: A Roman Catholic Lay Pastoral Care Model for the Use of Canine Companions in Ministry to the Elderly in Retirement Communities." Marylhurst University, 2002.

_____. "Four-Footed Ministers: Their Theology of Presence—a Research Study on CAM/PS (Canine-Assisted Ministry/Pastoral and Spiritual Care)." Marylhurst University, 2005.

_____. *Four-Footed Ministers: Their Theology of Presence.* Staarbrucken, Germany: VDM Verlag Dr. Muller e.K., 2008.

_____. "Do All Dogs Go to Heaven? Implications for Pastoral Care to Elder Persons." *Healing Ministry* 11, no. 2 (spring 2004): 77-80

_____. "The Significance of Story in Pastoral Care to the Elder Person." *Healing Ministry* 11, no. 3 (summer 2004): 113-115.

_____. "'If I but Touch the Hem of His Cloak . . .': 'Touching Prayer' as the Best of Both Worlds." *Healing Ministry* 13, no. 3 (summer 2006): 7-9.

_____. "Canine-Assisted Pastoral Care: She Gave a Party and Nobody Came." *Healing Ministry* 12, no. 1 (winter 2005): 13-16.

Fine, Aubrey H., ed. *Handbook on Animal-Assisted Therapy: Theoretical Foundations and Guidelines for Practice.* Burlington, MA: Academic Press, an imprint of Elsevier, 2010.

Linzey, Andrew. *Animal Theology.* Chicago: University of Illinois Press, 1995.

Webb, Stephen H. *On God and Dogs: A Christian Theology of Compassion for Animals.* New York: Oxford University Press, 1998.

Web Sites

* Pet Partners® (formerly the Delta Society): www.petpartners.org.
* The CDC Healthy Pets Healthy People: www.cdc.gov/healthypets/animals/dogs.htm.
* The CDC Healthy Pets Healthy People for health professionals: www.cdc.gov/healthypets/health_prof.htm.

APPENDIX B

PROGRAM FORMS

Exhibit A: MARYVILLE NURSING HOME

Additional Job Duties for Director
Connected with the Four-Footed Ministers Pastoral-Care Program
Based on Standard 2.4.1, 2.4.2, 2.4.3. *Standards of Practice for Animal-Assisted Activities and Animal-Assisted Therapy.* Bellevue, WA: Delta Society, 1996.
Approved: May 23, 2010

POSITION NAME: Director of Spiritual/   CLASSIFICATION: Exempt
Pastoral Services/Chaplain—FFMP Duties
LOCATION: Maryville Nursing Home   EFFECTIVE DATE: To Be Advised

GENERAL DUTIES BEYOND DIRECTOR'S JOB DESCRIPTION IN CONJUNCTION WITH FOUR-FOOTED MINISTERS PASTORAL-CARE PROGRAM: Because the Four-Footed Ministers Pastoral-Care Program integrates canine companions into a volunteer program of spiritual/pastoral care, it is important that additional duties be defined for the director of spiritual/pastoral services/chaplain position. This is necessary because of the specialized nature of this volunteer program.

ESSENTIAL ACTIVITIES/ RESPONSIBILITIES:

1. Attend educational activities on good practices running a safe, professional, and up-to-date animal-assisted intervention program.
2. Assist administration in the area of liability concerns with regard to the Four-Footed Ministers Pastoral-Care Program.
3. Continue education in good husbandry practices with regard to the safe and humane treatment of dogs in the spiritual/pastoral-care program.
4. In *collaboration with the FFMT program coordinator:*
   ❖ Assist in the development of goals and procedures for the program;
   ❖ Assist in the development and implementation of continual evaluation procedures to ensure that best practices are being followed with regard to the program;
   ❖ Assist in the development of methods for the integration of new volunteer teams in the spiritual/pastoral care visitation schedule;
   ❖ Assist in the review, termination, or release of under-performing teams or teams that no longer meet the minimum requirements for the program;
   ❖ Assist in the facilitation of problem resolution on issues involving Four-Footed Ministerial teams;
   ❖ Develop and conduct FFM team in-service and continuing-education seminars in spiritual/pastoral care for staff and volunteers;

- ❖ Help conduct monthly/as needed grief support meetings with FFM teams;
- ❖ With a veterinarian and FFMPC program coordinator, form an advisory committee to ensure the health and well-being of residents, staff, and volunteers and their dogs.

5. Educate staff, residents, and families as to the rationale, benefits, and risks of participating in the Four-Footed Ministers Pastoral-Care Program.
6. Advocate for the Four-Footed Ministers Pastoral-Care Program with the Board as the need arises.
7. Advocate for the Four-Footed Ministers Pastoral-Care Program outside of Maryville.

COMMUNICATION/RESIDENT CONTACT: per director's job description

SPECIFIC SKILLS REQUIRED: according to director's job description

EDUCATION AND/OR EXPERIENCE: according to director's job description.

JOB CONDITIONS: as per director's job description.

SUPERVISES: Four-Footed Ministers Pastoral-Care program coordinator.

Jerilyn E. Felton

Exhibit B: MARYVILLE NURSING HOME

Four-Footed Ministers Pastoral-Care Program Coordinator
FOUR-FOOTED MINISTERS PASTORAL-CARE PROGRAM
Based on Standard 2.4.1, 2.4.2, 2.4.3. *Standards of Practice for Animal-Assisted Activities and Animal-Assisted Therapy.* Bellevue, WA: Delta Society, 1996.
Approved May 23, 2010

POSITION NAME: FFMT Program Coordinator

CLASSIFICATION: Volunteer

LOCATION: Maryville Nursing Home

EFFECTIVE DATE: To Be Advised

GENERAL DUTIES IN THE FOUR-FOOTED MINISTERS PASTORAL-CARE PROGRAM:
The Four-Footed Ministers Pastoral-Care Program integrates canine companions into a volunteer program of spiritual/pastoral care. In collaboration with the director of spiritual/pastoral services/care, the FFMPC program coordinator develops, integrates, and supervises volunteer spiritual/pastoral-care provider teams that use dogs in ministry in one-on-one visits as well as dog-ministry prayer-group gatherings.

ESSENTIAL ACTIVITIES/ RESPONSIBILITIES:

1. Administer Four-Footed Ministers Pastoral-Care Program on behalf of the spiritual/pastoral-care department.
   - ❖ Assist the interdisciplinary team in the assessment of residents for participation in the Four-Footed Ministers Pastoral-Care Program.
   - ❖ Recruit, train, and supervise volunteer spiritual/pastoral-care provider teams.
   - ❖ Evaluate volunteers and their dogs for suitability for the Four-Footed Ministers Pastoral-Care Program.
   - ❖ Assist in assessment of contraindications in residents for participation in Four-Footed Ministers Pastoral-Care Program.
   - ❖ Be responsible for administrative tasks in running the program:
     - ❖ Maintain file of health records on dogs in the program;
     - ❖ Develop health requirements for FFM teams based on good practices for animal-assisted interventions;
     - ❖ Maintain FFMPC pastoral-care log file for program;
     - ❖ Register and credential FFM teams for visitation;
     - ❖ Schedule volunteer FFM teams for one-on-one visitation;
     - ❖ Schedule dog-ministry prayer-group gatherings;
     - ❖ Schedule FFM Team in-services and continuing-education sessions for staff and volunteers;
     - ❖ Assign volunteers to residents that request one-on-one visits;
     - ❖ Responsible for supplies for dogs in volunteer office;

74

❖ Update *Maryville Volunteer Handbook* section on FFM teams as needed;

❖ Develop and modify forms for the program.

2. Be knowledgeable about and integrate good practices running a safe, professional, and up-to-date animal-assisted intervention program.

3. Responsible for good husbandry practices with regard to the safe and humane treatment of dogs in the spiritual/pastoral-care program.

4. Assist director and administration in the area of liability concerns with regard to the Four-Footed Ministers Pastoral-Care Program.

5. *In collaboration with the director of spiritual/pastoral services/chaplain:*

❖ Assist in the development of goals and procedures for the program;

❖ Assist in the development and implementation of continual evaluation procedures to ensure that best practices are being followed with regard to the program;

❖ Assist in the development of methods for the integration of new volunteer teams in the spiritual/pastoral-care visitation schedule;

❖ Assist in the review, termination, or release of under-performing teams or teams that no longer meet the minimum requirements for the program;

❖ Assist in the facilitation of problem resolution on issues involving Four-Footed Ministerial teams;

❖ Assist in the development and running of FFM team in-services and continuing-education seminars in spiritual/pastoral care for staff and volunteers;

❖ Help conduct monthly/as needed grief support meetings with FFM teams;

❖ With a veterinarian and director of spiritual/pastoral services/chaplain, form an advisory committee to ensure the health and well-being of residents, staff, and volunteers and their dogs.

6. Educate staff, residents, and families as to the rationale, benefits, and risks of participating in the Four-Footed Ministers Pastoral-Care Program.

7. Promote the Four-Footed Ministers Pastoral-Care Program within and outside Maryville through presentations.

8. Serve as a community resource for the Four-Footed Ministers Pastoral-Care Program outside of Maryville.

9. Write and publish articles on the Four-Footed Ministers Pastoral-Care Program to update knowledge in the fields of animal-assisted interventions and spiritual/pastoral care.

10. Duties as assigned.

COMMUNICATION/RESIDENT CONTACT: This position requires that the FFMPC program coordinator work with staff, residents, and volunteers to ensure that all parties are safe at all times and that good practices are followed. As required, the FFMPC program coordinator will also work with the community to promote this form of ministry/pastoral care into other facilities.

SPECIFIC SKILLS REQUIRED: Excellent verbal and written communication skills, excellent customer service skills, the ability to be able to work with people from all walks of life, excellent organizational skills, and comprehensive knowledge of Microsoft Office are a minimum requirement for this position.

EDUCATION AND/OR EXPERIENCE: The ideal candidate should possess at least a Bachelor's degree in Theology or Theological Studies or a Certificate of Completion in Pastoral Care or Ministry as well as a have extensive knowledge of animal-assisted interventions as defined by Pet Partners® protocols and best practices.

JOB CONDITIONS: This position requires the volunteer to be on site and available when Four-Footed Ministerial teams are visiting or involved in dog-ministry prayer-group gatherings.

SUPERVISES: Volunteer Four-Footed Ministerial teams (volunteer and their dog).

Exhibit C: MARYVILLE NURSING HOME

Four-Footed Ministerial Team-Spiritual/Pastoral-Care Provider
FOUR-FOOTED MINISTERS PASTORAL-CARE PROGRAM
Based on Standard 2.4.1, 2.4.2, 2.4.3. *Standards of Practice for Animal-Assisted Activities and Animal-Assisted Therapy.* Bellevue, WA: Delta Society, 1996.
Date Formulated: August 10, 2010

POSITION NAME: Four-Footed Ministerial Team—**spiritual-care provider**

CLASSIFICATION: Volunteer

LOCATION: Maryville Nursing Home

EFFECTIVE DATE: To Be Advised

GENERAL DUTIES IN THE FOUR-FOOTED MINISTERS PASTORAL-CARE PROGRAM:
The Four-Footed Ministers Pastoral-Care Program integrates canine companions into a volunteer program of spiritual/pastoral care. The Four-Footed Ministerial Team consists of a volunteer **spiritual/pastoral-care provider** and their dog to be used in ministry in one-on-one visits as well as dog-ministry prayer-group gatherings.

ESSENTIAL ACTIVITIES/ RESPONSIBILITIES:

1. Assist the pastoral-care department in providing spiritual/pastoral care and comfort to residents, their family members, and staff of Maryville.
    ❖ Be knowledgeable in Pet Partners® protocols and best practices of animal-assisted interventions.
    ❖ Advise the FFMPC program coordinator if a resident, after a visit, exhibits contraindications for participation in Four-Footed Ministers Pastoral-Care Program.
    ❖ Follow all protocols and procedures as outlined in the *Maryville Volunteer Handbook* for volunteer interactions and those defined by the FFMPC program:
        ❖ Provide health records on dog(s) to the FFMPC program coordinator;
        ❖ Follow health requirements for FFM teams based on good practices for animal-assisted interventions;
        ❖ Sign in and sign out; make entries in FFMPC Log;
        ❖ Be credentialed as an FFM team for visitation;
        ❖ Advise the FFMPC program coordinator at least 24 hours before scheduled time if unable to make a scheduled one-on-one visit or dog-ministry prayer-group gathering;
        ❖ Keep Pet Partners® registration/certification current on the dog registered in the program and provide record of such compliance;
        ❖ Be familiar with Maryville's policies and procedures—especially those relating to confidentiality;
        ❖ Be able to assess stress in residents and dogs taking appropriate action;
        ❖ Practice safety at all times.
2. Be responsible for good husbandry practices with regard to the safe and humane treatment of dogs in the spiritual/pastoral-care program.

3. With the FFMPC program coordinator, assist, as able, to facilitate problem resolution on issues involving Four-Footed Ministerial teams.
4. Attend FFM team in-services and continuing-education seminars in spiritual/pastoral care.
5. Attend, pet-grief support meetings, if need be.
6. Act as ambassador to the community on behalf of the Four-Footed Ministers Pastoral-Care Program.

COMMUNICATION/RESIDENT CONTACT: This position requires the volunteer to be able to interact will all types of people—residents, family members, and staff—while acting in a safe and pastoral manner.

Exhibit D: MARYVILLE NURSING HOME

Four-Footed Ministerial Team—Volunteer
FOUR-FOOTED MINISTERS PASTORAL-CARE PROGRAM
Based on Standard 2.4.1, 2.4.2, 2.4.3. *Standards of Practice for Animal-Assisted Activities and Animal-Assisted Therapy.* Bellevue, WA: Delta Society, 1996.
Approved: May 23, 2010; Revised: August 10, 2010

POSITION NAME: Four-Footed Ministerial CLASSIFICATION: Volunteer
Team—**volunteer**
LOCATION: Maryville Nursing Home   EFFECTIVE DATE: To Be Advised

GENERAL DUTIES IN THE FOUR-FOOTED MINISTERS PASTORAL-CARE PROGRAM:
The Four-Footed Ministers Pastoral-Care Program integrates canine companions into a volunteer program of spiritual/pastoral care. The Four-Footed Ministerial Team consists of a volunteer and their dog to be used **as support for spiritual/pastoral care staff** in one-on-one visits as well as dog-ministry prayer-group gatherings.

ESSENTIAL ACTIVITIES/ RESPONSIBILITIES:

1. Assist the spiritual/pastoral-care department in providing pastoral/spiritual care and comfort to residents, their family members, and staff of Maryville. **This position parallels the role played by Pet Partners®-registered teams for animal-assisted therapy.**
   - ❖ Be knowledgeable in Pet Partners® protocols and best practices of animal-assisted interventions.
   - ❖ Follow all protocols and procedures as outlined in the *Maryville Volunteer Handbook* with regard to volunteer interactions and those specific to the FFMPC program:
     - ❖ Provide health records on dog to the FFMPC program coordinator;
     - ❖ Follow health requirements for FFM teams based on good practices for animal-assisted interventions;
     - ❖ Sign in and sign out;
     - ❖ Be credentialed as an FFM Team for visitation;
     - ❖ Advise the FFMPC program coordinator at least 24 hours before scheduled time if unable to make a scheduled one-on-one visit or dog-ministry prayer-group gathering;
     - ❖ Keep Pet Partners® registration/certification current on the dog registered in the program and provide record of such compliance;
     - ❖ Be familiar with Maryville's policies and procedures—especially those relating to confidentiality;
     - ❖ Practice safety at all times.
2. Be responsible for good husbandry practices with regard to the safe and humane treatment of the dog.

Optional attendance beyond initial volunteer training session: Attend FFM team in-services and continuing-education seminars in spiritual/pastoral care sessions.

3. Act as ambassador to the community on behalf of the Four-Footed Ministers Pastoral-Care Program.

COMMUNICATION/RESIDENT CONTACT: This position requires the volunteer to be able to interact will all types of people—residents, family members, and staff—while acting in a safe manner.

Exhibit E: Sample Ads

For Web Site

Maryville, a nursing home facility with approximately 150 residents located in Beaverton, Oregon, is looking for Pet Partners® teams to work in "dog ministry." Pet Partners® teams will have the option to function as assistants in spiritual animal-assisted therapy or to move beyond these interactions to directly assist the Four-Footed Ministers Pastoral-Care program coordinator and/or chaplain in the spiritual/pastoral care of residents, families, and staff.

It is dog teams that are needed. Basic training in spiritual/pastoral care will be provided.

Please contact: Sister Josephine Pelster (maryville@ssmoministries.org), Spiritual/ Pastoral Care Services at 503-643-8626.

For Newsletter Ad
Marysville Nursing Home, Beaverton, OR

Maryville is a nursing-home facility with approximately 150 residents located in Beaverton, Oregon that is looking for Pet Partners® teams to be involved dog ministry to individuals and groups. Pet Partners® teams have the option to function as 'spiritual' therapy dogs with the FFMPC program coordinator and/or a board-certified chaplain who offers spiritual/pastoral care and comfort. This volunteer position is similar to working with professionals or paraprofessionals in AAT. If the team wishes, they have the option to move beyond 'spiritual' AAT interactions and become spiritual-care providers offering spiritual and pastoral care directly to residents, families, and staff. Basic training in spiritual/pastoral care will be provided.

Exhibit F: Sample Application

**MARYVILLE NURSING HOME
FOUR-FOOTED MINISTERS PASTORAL-CARE PROGRAM
APPLICATION**
Approved May 23, 2010

POSITION NAME: Four-Footed Ministerial Team

CLASSIFICATION: Volunteer

START DATE:

APPLICATION RECEIVED:

INTERVIEW COMPLETED:

NAME: _____ ANIMAL COMPANION: _____

ADDRESS _____

CITY/STATE/ZIP: _____

PHONE: _____ EMAIL: _____

EMERGENCY CONTACT: _____

PHONE: _____

DOCUMENTS NEEDED TO SUPPORT APPLICATION:

Pet Partners Registration Confirmation: _____ Received: _____

Pet Partners Health Screening Form: _____ Received: _____

Pet Partners Volunteer Agreement: _____ Received: _____

Copy of Recent Vaccinations on Pet: _____ Received: _____

The Four-Footed Ministers Pastoral-Care Program is a volunteer program of spiritual/ pastoral care offered to the residents of Maryville Nursing Home that provides care and comfort through the ministerial presence of a volunteer and their dog. In addition to the high ethical standards that have been set by Pet Partners®, Bellevue, Washington, the Four-Footed Ministers Pastoral-Care Program fulfills the mission of the Sisters of St. Mary of Oregon to offer "Service with Love." It is expected that those who volunteer will exhibit the highest ethical conduct in accordance with Pet Partners® ethical directives as well as abide by the standards of conduct outlined in the *Maryville Volunteer Handbook*.

After submitting this application, going through an initial interview, and completing the Four-Footed Ministers Pastoral-Care Program training, I, the undersigned, agree to abide by Pet Partners® protocols as well as the volunteer policies and procedures defined in the *Maryville Volunteer Handbook*.

_____   _____
Signature of Volunteer   Signature of Director
                                                              or FFMPC Program Coordinator

Exhibit G: Sample Lesson Plans for Training a Group of Volunteers/Spiritual-Care Providers

Preliminary Questions for Preparing Training Sessions

These are questions that volunteers might ask and can be good conversation starters:

- ❖ Why did you want to participate in this ministry?
- ❖ What do you need to know about our facility that will make this a great experience for you?
- ❖ What kind of expectations to you have for your volunteer work in the Four-Footed Ministers Pastoral—Care Program?

First Training Session

Begin with Prayer

Self-Introductions—using questions listed above as starters; this is a chance for team members get to know each other.

Sister Josephine will discuss important Maryville policies from the *Maryville Volunteer Handbook*, including check-in for FFM teams

- ❖ Boundaries
- ❖ Confidentiality
- ❖ Hand-washing or alcohol lotion
- ❖ Respecting privacy: HIPPAA regulations
- ❖ Respecting choices and diverse spiritualties
- ❖ Maryville's Volunteer application and confidentiality form

Tour of facility follows with emphasis on special needs of the dogs, the check-in/out area, FFMPC pastoral-care log (if used), disposal areas, potty areas, etc.

- ❖ Volunteer office
- ❖ Center Unit
- ❖ Courtyard
- ❖ West Unit and area outside of business office
- ❖ Alzheimer's Unit
- ❖ Chapel

Break

The dog ministry component—Jerilyn to offer a PowerPoint presentation that explains the story of the ministry model and outlines the steps for visitation.

Second Training Session

Begin with Prayer

Sharing the Story—volunteers share their stories about their Pet Partners® experiences in visitation in other areas

Break

Spiritual/Pastoral Care Skills—Sister Josephine will present the following:

- ❖ Attentive listening to the story
- ❖ Literal
- ❖ Emotional: verbal and non-verbal
- ❖ Meaning: is there a story within this story?
- ❖ Spiritual: how is God (or Higher Power) present?
- ❖ Self-care: intuition increases in the elderly as hearing, comprehending, and vision decrease. The elderly person's gifts and challenges are accentuated. Sister will provide examples.
- ❖ Volunteers should be present in the moment giving the other person time to take the lead in the conversation.
- ❖ Volunteers should aim for establishing a trusting relationship; repeating information is often necessary. The volunteer should share briefly about him/herself, building a bridge in connecting with the resident. Volunteers should keep their story short; there will be time later in the relationship for more of the volunteer's story to be shared.
- ❖ In being with grief it is important to listen . . . listen . . . listen; affirm the resident's loss as mourning the loss of a pet is healthy. Sister will review manifestations of normal grief and the tasks of the bereaved.

Multi-tasking in spiritual/pastoral-care using a dog: Jerilyn will address these challenges that are unique to multi-tasking in spiritual/pastoral-care using a dog.

Finding the "We"—Sister, Jerilyn, Four-Footed Ministerial teams discuss how to work together in dog ministry at Maryville.

*Exhibit H: Sections from the Maryville Nursing Home
Volunteer Handbook, pages 7-8*

Volunteer Requirements for Four-Footed Ministers Pastoral-Care Program

Maryville has begun a program of volunteer spiritual care using dogs. This program aims to provide spiritual and pastoral comfort to those who love dogs, have had dogs as pets, and have no medical reason why they cannot interact with dogs. The Four-Footed Ministerial team acts as an extension of the pastoral-care office and volunteer observations are important to the chaplain who takes seriously their assessment of a resident's well-being. Thus, the Four-Footed Ministerial teams form an important part of the overall spiritual and pastoral care of not only the resident, but also the staff and the families who visit.

While many individuals have dogs and often want to use them in spiritual and pastoral care, in order to ensure the safety of all concerned—residents, staff, and the volunteer—only Pet Partners®-registered dog teams are permitted in the program. If this type of volunteer ministry appeals to you, please contact the Four-Footed Pastoral-Care program coordinator for more information about Pet Partners® registration.

Sign in: Upon arriving, please sign in at the reception desk and in the volunteer office. The Four-Footed Ministers Pastoral-Care program coordinator will be on site and accompany you as you visit the residents. If you are an FFM team "volunteer" you will be the advocate for your dog, working with the FFMPC program coordinator who will function as the spiritual-care provider.

The Visit: Though prayer and spiritual comfort is the aim of these visits, interactions with Pet Partners® teams will have many positive results and these might not be immediately apparent. If you have any concerns, please discuss them with the FFMPC program coordinator or the chaplain.

Name Tags:. Please have your Maryville and Pet Partners® name tags with you and prominently displayed. You must wear the Maryville name tag at all times while in the facility. There will be blue smocks available for you to wear over your clothes if you wish.

Sign out: At the conclusion of your visit, please sign out in the volunteer office and at reception.

Last-Minute Emergencies: If you are unable to come when scheduled, or have any questions or concerns, please inform the FFMPC program coordinator. A 24-hour notice of non-attendance is greatly appreciated.

SECTION FOUR: VOLUNTEER INFORMATION
Volunteer Job Descriptions (pg. 12)
(The following list contains ideas for volunteers)

Adopt a Grandparent: Provide companionship to a few residents, or just one on a regular basis.

Arts and Crafts: Individually or helping a facilitator with a group of residents.

Beauty Time: Nail care, hair, and makeup: group or individually.

Book/Poetry Reading: Small groups, or individual reading.

Entertainment: Music, plays, singing, church groups, school groups, music programs, dance programs.

Feeding Program: Helping those residents who need assistance. Training required.

**Four-Footed Ministers Pastoral-Care Program: in conjunction with the director of spiritual/pastoral services and the Four-Footed Ministers Pastoral-Care program coordinator, provide spiritual and pastoral comfort to residents and their families. Specialized training is required to participate with one's dog.

Games: Cards, board games, Bingo, puzzles, and more.

Groups Visits: Churches, schools, Scouts, etc. Monthly visits or helping with special events.

Facilitation: Leaders who will facilitate, or help activity staff with a group of residents in an activity or special program.

Outings: Helping the activity staff escort residents out of the facility for special outings, such as the beach, fishing, Beaverton parade, and restaurants.

*Pet Visitation: In addition to the Four-Footed Ministers Pastoral-Care Program, we have a program of dog visitation that is provided by Pet Partners®-registered teams.

Transport: Helping transport residents to and from activities and mass.

Teach: Sharing your special skills and talents with residents, either individually or in a group setting.

Exhibit I: Sample of Four-Footed Ministers Pastoral Care Log

Four-Footed Ministers Pastoral Care Log

Date	Name of FFMT	Room#	Status of Resident Visited									
			In a good mood; cheerful	Easy eye contact with both FFMT and dog	Opened up to FFM Team (s) and told stories	Neutral	Did not seem to want a visit	Easily Distracted— remaining distracted	Restless anxious nervous	Did not want to interact as had in past	Withdrawn —sad	Hostile to FFMT
			In a good mood; cheerful	Easy eye contact with both FFMT and dog	Opened up to FFM Team (s) and told stories	Neutral	Did not seem to want a visit	Easily Distracted— remaining distracted	Restless anxious nervous	Did not want to interact as had in past	Withdrawn —sad	Hostile to FFMT
			In a good mood; cheerful	Easy eye contact with both FFMT and dog	Opened up to FFM Team (s) and told stories	Neutral	Did not seem to want a visit	Easily Distracted— remaining distracted	Restless anxious nervous	Did not want to interact as had in past	Withdrawn —sad	Hostile to FFMT
			In a good mood; cheerful	Easy eye contact with both FFMT and dog	Opened up to FFM Team (s) and told stories	Neutral	Did not seem to want a visit	Easily Distracted— remaining distracted	Restless anxious nervous	Did not want to interact as had in past	Withdrawn —sad	Hostile to FFMT
			In a good mood; cheerful	Easy eye contact with both FFMT and dog	Opened up to FFM Team (s) and told stories	Neutral	Did not seem to want a visit	Easily Distracted— remaining distracted	Restless anxious nervous	Did not want to interact as had in past	Withdrawn —sad	Hostile to FFMT
			In a good mood; cheerful	Easy eye contact with both FFMT and dog	Opened up to FFM Team (s) and told stories	Neutral	Did not seem to want a visit	Easily Distracted— remaining distracted	Restless anxious nervous	Did not want to interact as had in past	Withdrawn —sad	Hostile to FFMT
	Notes For Chaplain											

The above chart highlights descriptions of possible resident reactions and provides an easy way for the Four-Footed Ministerial team to record the status of the resident. If there are concerns about the welfare of the resident, notes can be made for the chaplain/director for further follow-up. The chaplain/director will make notes in the resident's chart and alert other senior staff to the concerns noticed by the Four-Footed Ministerial team.

Exhibit J: Sample of Four-Footed Ministers Assessment Tool

Four-Footed Ministers Assessment Tool

Date	Name of FFMT	Room#	Visitation
	Notes For Chaplain		

This more complex form could be used in much the same manner as the Four-Footed Ministers pastoral-care log but should be utilized by a more experienced spiritual/pastoral-care provider. Its function is to alert the chaplain/director to specific concerns that surfaced in a visit. The chaplain/director can then follow-up with senior staff and/or make notations in the patient's/resident's chart.

APPENDIX C:

DOG MINISTRY PRAYER-GROUP GATHERINGS

Examples based on the book, *The Master's Companion: A Christian Midrash*

Exhibit A: Dog-Ministry Prayer-Group Gathering

Date: Began January 27, 2011
Note Date: January 27, 2011—The quality of compassion

General Comments: As this had been advertised within the facility, the group consisted of more than those who have been participating in the study. The comments made and reported in this summary reflect only those who have signed an informed consent form. We had a total of seven attendees, one husband and wife with several other residents including two who are participating in the study—Judith[3] and Sean.

Service as Designed		Service as Conducted (Taken from an actual gathering)
Call to Prayer	With individuals seated in a circle: begin with "Let us all be in God's Spirit, and we begin this time of prayer and meditation in the name of the Holy One."	We began with this prayer. It was not a smooth introduction because one of the residents was vocalizing and Sister Josephine thought it best to take that resident out of the group. After she left, we continued with the prayer. At this point, I[4] gave a short introduction of what would happen during our gathering.
Silence	Time for centering and connecting to Spirit.	There was not too much time for this. We had individuals who continually joined our group as they discovered the dogs in the center of the gathering.

---

3   If a name is indicated, that person agreed to be in the study. The use of a letter indicates that the person was not in the study but attended.

4   The 'I' indicated in these summaries is the researcher.

Service as Designed		Service as Conducted (Taken from an actual gathering)
Welcome:	"Welcome to the circle of wisdom where we can share our stories of our canine companions and other beloved animals learning lessons of life from their interactions with us. Today's lesson is that of compassion. "We begin with a mystery. A musty document has come across the desk of an academic who sees that it tells a story about Jesus not found in the Gospels. The story seems to answer the question, 'What if Jesus had a pet dog?' This story is based on the method used by the rabbis in the Jewish tradition where they, being great storytellers who were filled with the Word of God, filled in the blanks left in the approved scripture stories. This story uses imagination to fill in the blanks left in the Gospel stories. "Since Jesus loved those who were outcasts from society, it seems logical that he would also take in outcasts from the animal world, dogs for example. Dogs were outcast because of they were scavengers and fed on blood, an act that was forbidden according to the Jewish law. "What follows is the story about Jesus and a dog that found a place in the community of disciples."	I followed this outline, pointing out the lesson of compassion that would be illustrated in the reading of the story. I briefly summarized the story's "Prologue" and then moved on to the question that the book addresses—"What if Jesus had a pet dog?" I did not share this information with the group as I was not sure how it would be received. I felt it was too academic for our first gathering. As I will have to go back many times to catch up those who had not heard the story from the beginning, I will have time to cover this information at some point, depending on the mix of who attends.
Scriptural Reading	Read "Prologue" and "Chapter 1" of *The Master's Companion.* Adjust the amount read contingent on the situation at the time.	I summarized much of the story, reading only the first part of Chapter 1. This seemed to provide a natural break. I read pages 17-19.
Silence	A period for reflection.	I skipped this short silence because I wanted to see what would happen when we opened the floor to personal stories.

Service as Designed		Service as Conducted (Taken from an actual gathering)
Faith sharing time on Compassion	Time for sharing of stories about past experiences where each resident had a chance to be compassionate to an outcast animal.	I asked Barbara [ministry partner] to share a story so that she could model for the group what sharing might look like. She told a wonderful story of how she picked up a loose dog when she was on an errand. She wanted to make sure that the dog would be returned to its rightful owner. Her story illustrated the quality of compassion that was the theme for this chapter. Many of the attendees then shared their stories and Judith shared her story of her Four-Footed Minister mutt that she and her husband took to an "old folk's home" to visit. Judith had not trained the dog but the dog seemed to know what to do. The dog would go to each person and acted appropriately as if she had been trained. Another woman participant shared her story of taking in a dog that was going to be dumped by someone. She showed compassion for the dog not wanting it to be left to fend for itself. It all began because Barbara modeled the behavior for our residents. Given the importance of knowing how to respond, points to the fact that Four-Footed Ministers need to go in pairs—one helping the other if the situation warrants.
Next Session	A Night in the Garden (Chapter 2)—Jesus is our refuge from fear.	I briefly mentioned that the story would continue in two weeks.
Conclusion: Sending Forth	Let us now pray . . . "Holy One, as we reflect on the beauty of your creation, let us take the lessons we have learned into our community to spread Your joy, Your love, and Your peace. Amen"	I gave this short blessing and we concluded the prayer service. Though Sean came in at this point, I asked this individual who had had ministerial training to bless the participants. He not only blessed the participants but also blessed the dogs, wishing them long life.

Exhibit B: Dog-Ministry Prayer-Group Gathering

Chapter 2

Note Date: February 10, 2011-A Lesson on freedom from fear.

Prior to our beginning our prayer service, Jael and Judith were in our small room talking with me about Alya. Judith observed how important dogs were to her and she continued to talk to Alya using 'motherese,' language that mothers use with their young children. Her insights as to the importance of dogs were very surprising given her past encounters with us.

Jael is a dear woman who is a very shy person yet could engage with the conversation about dogs and how much she liked them. When Joseph entered, he commented again on how Alya's eyes 'took in' the person on whom her gaze rested. G. commented that Alya's eyes did, in fact engage him greatly. Abigail confirmed that Alya's eyes were an important part of her personality, showing the love she has for me and others.

For this gathering, we joined by two other individuals, G. and P., who are not in the study.

Service as Designed		Service as Conducted
Call to Prayer	With individuals seated in a circle: begin with "Let us all be in God's Spirit, and we begin this time of prayer and meditation in the name of the Holy One."	I shortened this call to prayer just slightly as I was not sure what faith traditions we had present, but did ask God to be present to our group.
Silence	Time for centering and connecting to Spirit.	In order to keep our group engaged as sleep often gets the best of them, I kept this very short, allowing time for silence in the span of taking a deep breath.

Service as Designed		Service as Conducted
Welcome:	"Welcome back to our circle of wisdom where we can share our stories of our canine companions and other beloved animals by sharing the lessons they have taught us. Today's lesson is that of freedom from fear. Remember our story began with a mystery where Dr. Evelyn Brown received a musty document from the First Century A.D. She discovered that it told a story about Jesus, not found in the Gospels. The story seems to answer the question, 'What if Jesus had a pet dog?' "In our first chapter, we met Sarah, the Samaritan woman who took in Jesus and the disciples and fed them. As the whole community wanted to see Jesus, they gathered outside of Sarah's house after dinner. The small black dog with the white foot came into the gathering that caused the community members to be afraid. They were afraid of the dog because dogs were outcasts. Jesus had been telling a story about a loyal sheepdog, and there a dog appeared. Jesus spoke quietly and reached out to the dog and to the community by calming their fears. "Today we read about what happened during the two days that Jesus spent in the village. This chapter will show us Jesus and the disciples confronting both a physical and spiritual threat."	I tried to summarize the story, going back to fill in the gaps that occurred in the first gathering, as I want to keep the reading to a minimum and concentrate more on telling the story.

Service as Designed		Service as Conducted
Scriptural Reading	Read Chapter 2. "A Night in the Garden" of *The Master's Companion.*	After summarizing the story to this point, I read the short passage where Merea confronts an evil presence and alerts Jesus and the disciples. This is only a small section of Chapter 2 (pages 36-39) but reading it moved the group to consider the theme for the day that was freedom from fear. All of the individuals seemed to be engaged in the story for I could tell how attentive they were through eye contact. Alya continued to snooze at the center of the group that had been crammed into the small gathering space. This did facilitate connection because this way everyone could hear and see me without straining.
Silence	A period for reflection.	I went immediately into the next section of sharing pet stories. I asked Sister Josephine to go first so that she could model for the group a story about a pet protecting us just as Jesus protects us from harm.
Faith sharing time on freedom from fear	Time for sharing of stories about past experiences where each resident talked about how the companionship of their animal helped them to calm their fears about something that threatened them such as a person, a situation, etc.	No one else shared stories at this time.
Next Session	Jesus and the Canaanite Woman (Chapter 3) where a person pays it forward.	
Conclusion: Sending Forth	Let us now pray . . . "Almighty God, as we reflect on the beauty of your creation, let us take the lessons we have learned into our community to spread Your joy, Your love, and Your peace. Amen"	I concluded with this brief prayer as lunch was going to be served at noon. Our service lasted about 20 minutes. Everyone seemed to enjoy the story.

After our gathering I sat with Joseph and Abigail. Joseph shared another story about a dog's compassion and courage. As he said he lived in Beaverton for 38 years, he remembered a time when he saw a family of five ahead of him on a walk to a local park. One of the children had a dog on a rope that was ahead of the other family members, when the younger sister of about five years of age missed the pedal on her bike and slipped to the ground crying. The dog ran back to comfort the child, staying with her until she stopped crying.

When Sister and I debriefed after this session, Sister mentioned that Joseph's stories focused on incidents in his life that showed forth God's protection and love. They were significant events where God had broken through to show his kindness and compassion.

Notes from March 17, 2011:

In our debriefing with Sister Josephine we determined that:

1. We will meet in the hall outside of the chapel to give us more space. It will be an intimate but not a confining space lit by natural light. [Note that this has not been possible.]
2. Barbara suggested I pose the question for the group earlier in our gathering before I read the scripture/story. She suggested I phrase it in simpler language so that the participants can understand what I am asking them to consider.
3. Barbara asked how we might connect to a woman who attends but is language-challenged. We will need to figure a way to help her feel more comfortable in the group.
4. I will email Sister the scriptural verses for the subsequent week's story so that those who are still able to read can prepare themselves for the gathering.

APPENDIX D

MARYVILLE PROTOCOLS FOR FOUR-FOOTED
MINISTERS PASTORAL-CARE PROGRAM

Vision Statement

The Four-Footed Ministers Pastoral-Care Program presents the opportunity to volunteer Pet Partners® teams, consisting of a volunteer and their dog, to provide spiritual/pastoral care to residents, their families, and staff through the gift of their presence and loving service.

❖ Only Pet Partners®-registered teams, consisting of an approved volunteer and their dog, are eligible for the Four-Footed Ministers Pastoral-Care Program. For more information on the registration process, please visit Pet Partners® website at www. petpartners.org.

❖ The Four-Footed Ministers Pastoral-Care program coordinator will keep up-to-date records on all visiting teams designated as "volunteers" or spiritual-care providers. These records will consist of an application for the program, a signed job description, current Pet Partners® registration, and current health records for the dog.

❖ The "volunteer" and/or spiritual-care provider is subject to Maryville volunteer requirements that include a background check (See Appendix B for separate job descriptions). There are no special health tests that are required.

❖ All "volunteer" and spiritual-care providers are required to attend orientation and training sessions prior to beginning their ministry work. Occasional debriefing sessions will be held in order to check in with teams as the need arises.

❖ All Pet Partners® requirements for visitation are to be followed unless they specifically conflict with Maryville volunteer policies and procedures. At this time, there are no conflicts. If questions arise, Four-Footed Ministerial teams can refer the matter to the FFMPC program coordinator for clarification.

❖ Four-Footed Ministerial teams are required to sign in at both the reception desk and the volunteer office.

❖ As Maryville is a relatively "open" campus, the Four-Footed Ministerial teams are free to move about the halls interacting with residents, family members, and staff unless otherwise directed. The only volunteer shift that has been routinely scheduled for ministry is held on Thursdays beginning at 10 a.m. and concluding at noon. Normally, the dog-ministry prayer-group gatherings are scheduled at 11 a.m. in the small visitors' room. As more teams become involved, more visitation times can be scheduled.

❖ If a person is actively involved in ministry and has had spiritual/pastoral care —experience working with elders, such as a member of the clergy or an ordained minister, that person is designated as a spiritual/pastoral-care provider. This individual is able to call on residents without the FFMPC program coordinator or chaplain accompanying them. This person must alert the FFMPC program coordinator well in advance as to the time and day they wish come. A follow-up report is required for this activity.

❖ The Visit: Though prayer and spiritual comfort are the aims of these visits, interactions with Pet Partners® teams will have many positive results that might not be immediately apparent. If a volunteer has any concerns please discuss them with the FFMPC program coordinator or the chaplain.

* Name Tags: It is required that the Maryville and Pet Partners® name tags be prominently displayed. All volunteers must also wear the Maryville name tag at all times while in the facility.

* The FFMPC program coordinator will make available to Four-Footed Ministerial teams a list of those who have requested spiritual/pastoral care visits. It will be posted on the volunteer log in the volunteer office on visitation day noting the number of the room/bed of the person requesting a spiritual/pastoral-care visit.

* Each Four-Footed Ministerial team must sign out both at the reception desk and the volunteer office before leaving campus. If there are any concerns that surfaced in a visit, the volunteer office has forms that can be used to alert the FFMPC program coordinator and/or chaplain to those concerns.

* Last-Minute Emergencies: If an emergency arises, or a volunteer has any questions or concerns, please inform the FFMPC program coordinator. A 24-hour notice of non-attendance is greatly appreciated.

* As in any dealings with animals, there are times when accidents do happen. It is important that if an accident occurs, the volunteer alert one of the nursing staff, who will prepare the Maryville Resident Incident Report. The Four-Footed Ministerial team should work the FFMPC program coordinator to fill out the appropriate form for submission to Pet Partners®.

* As safety and the overall good of the residents are the primary concern of Maryville staff and the volunteers, there might be times when a Four-Footed Ministerial team should not continue to visit. This matter will be brought to the attention of the FFMPC program coordinator and chaplain who will meet with the "volunteer" or spiritual-care provider to discuss the matter and take appropriate action.

* Finally, it is important that each Four-Footed Ministerial team enjoy the experience of sharing their caring concern and the gift of their canine companion with those who love dogs and want to interact with them. Maryville wishes all volunteer teams in the Four-Footed Ministers Pastoral-Care Program every blessing for this holy work.

APPENDIX E

MARYVILLE FFMPC PROGRAM TRAINING MODULE SAMPLE

Sample of Staff Training Presentation/Volunteer
and Spiritual-Care Presentation

SLIDE 1

SCRIPT: Thank you for attending this session today that will inform you about a new form of canine care here at Maryville. This new ministry is the Four-Footed Ministers Pastoral-Care Program. This ministry formed the basis for a Master's thesis and a Master's project. The Master's thesis, completed in 2002, laid the theological and theoretical groundwork for the research project conducted in 2004. The 2004 research project used the CAM/PS model that will be explained later. Further, the CAM/PS model is the basis for additional research completed at Maryville where a training manual on the concept was developed. The training manual is designed for directors of spiritual/pastoral care in nursing-care facilities so that they can "duplicate" Maryville's successes.

So, to begin, let's look at some of the basics.

SLIDE 2

"PET THERAPY" DEFINED
THE CONCEPTS

Animal-Assisted Activity:

"Meet and Greet" modality.

Animal-Assisted Therapy:

Interactions with the dog are specifically directed to measurable therapeutic outcomes.

CAM/PS: Falls in the middle adding the spiritual piece.

Photo by Kathryn K. Conrow, 2007

SCRIPT: You might have heard the term "pet therapy" in connection with animals in healthcare settings. This popular term is more correctly broken down into animal-assisted activities and animal-assisted therapy, which are lumped together under the term "animal-assisted interventions." To understand the CAM/PS model, there are distinctions that are important when defining the treatment modality, i.e., animal-assisted therapy, from mere beneficial interactions with a canine, i.e., animal-assisted activities.

Animal-assisted activity can be defined as "meet and greet" action where a resident or staff member interacts with the dog with no measurable therapeutic goals in mind. *For example: family members who visit with their dog, who interacts with residents and staff.*

Animal-assisted therapy, on the other hand, is defined as the modality where a canine and owner/handler are part of a treatment plan for a person. The interactions with the dog are specifically directed to measurable therapeutic goals set by a professional or a para-professional. *For example, having a resident brush the dog to recover arm strength after a stroke required by a treatment plan and specified as a measurable and documented goal.*

CAM/PS lies in between animal-assisted activity and animal-assisted therapy.

SLIDE 3

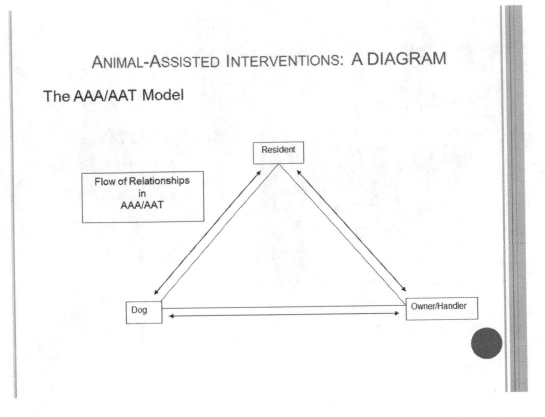

SCRIPT: Here is a physical representation of how the parties interact in animal-assisted interventions. There are a couple of things to note in this diagram:

The foundation for the relationships is the established connection of the owner/handler to the dog. There must be a firm hierarchical connection where the dog submits to the owner in unquestioned obedience. Moreover, the relationship is one of trust, where the dog trusts the owner to command what is best for the team. The relationship to the resident or staff member is built on the connection of dog to owner/handler. Further, the relationship to the resident or staff member can be established if that person does not fear dogs or has had a bad experience with them.

The relationship between dog and resident can be cemented because of the dog's natural tendency to express unconditional acceptance of human beings, regardless of their appearance or condition. Moreover, the dog's physical makeup: being soft, warm, and furry, possessing large eyes and wagging tale—presents an invitation that most humans cannot resist.

SLIDE 4

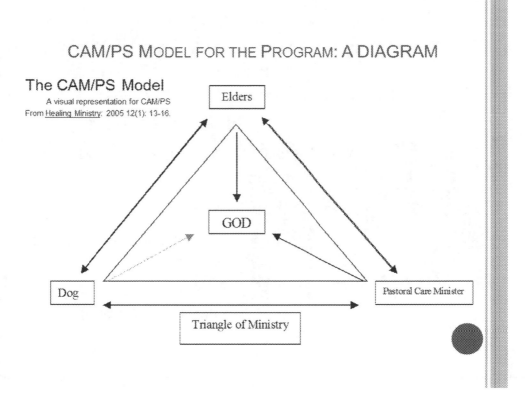

SCRIPT: The CAM/PS model builds on the natural interaction of humans and dogs. There are a couple of things to note in this diagram:

Here, the triangle expresses how loving kindness can flow among the participants on another level. The spiritual-care minister has the primary relationship with the dog as caregiver and, again, this relationship forms the basis of the triangle. The other relationships are initially facilitated by the physical interactions of the parties. Touch is the key to this interaction and is particularly valuable in a nursing-care facility. The spiritual relationship to God in the center can then be built and/or strengthened.

The relationship of the dog to God is drawn in red with a dotted line because this relationship is not yet been defined.

This whole scheme is based on a theology that sees all sentient beings as participating in God's life connected to each other horizontally as fellow creatures as well as vertically, following a traditional interpretation found in Genesis. The CAM/PS model of relationships reflects the circular chain of being.

SLIDE 5

FOUR-FOOTED MINISTERS PASTORAL-CARE PROGRAM
A RESEARCH STUDY ON CAM/PS (2004)

Project Particulars:

1. Population – Independent Elders

2. Venue – Parish

3. Methodology – theological reflection

4. Results – Most thought dogs help prayer life.

Photo by Kathryn K. Conrow, 2007

SCRIPT: To test the CAM/PS model, independent elder volunteers were invited to participate in a series of prayer-service/faith-sharing sessions conducted in a parish setting. These elder parish members were encouraged to share their stories about their pets seen in the light of a reflection upon scriptural passages that specifically related to animals. The connecting thread for each of the scripture passages chosen was a quality that could or had been be attributed to the Divine, e.g., loyalty. Heidi, the Four-Footed Minister engaged for the study, was on a long lead and able to engage at will with the participants as she wished. Moreover, she was available to be petted by the participants as they saw fit.

"Success" was determined by the stories told; a methodology used in spiritual/pastoral care-research studies. The results confirmed that most elders could see the connection of their pet stories and scripture that led to a more prayerful interaction with God. They had not thought of scripture, their pet stories, or God in that way before.

SLIDE 6

FOUR-FOOTED MINISTERS PASTORAL-CARE PROGRAM
THE FOUR-FOOTED MEMBER

The Requirements to Conduct Research using a Dog

1. Trained to respond to basic obedience commands.

2. Dog had predictable behavior to minimize risk of accidents.

3. Dog had "documented" health checks, shots and heartworm/flea control medications.

4. **Registered by a Pet Partner® trainer**, through Pet Partners® (OHS).

Why Registration was Important:

Protection for team and organization where ministry conducted. Liability insurance of up to $2,000,000 covers a Pet Partner ® team during their volunteer activities.

Alya
Kathryn K. Conrow 2007

SCRIPT: For the 2004 study, the first step was to engage a team covered by liability insurance for the one big concern was the risk of accidents. In the study, the Four-Footed Ministerial team was composed of Ms. Becky Rodes, an occupational therapist, and Heidi, her five-year-old English Springer spaniel. Heidi was trained to respond to basic commands and exhibit predictable behavior. She was current on her shots and was on medications for fleas and heartworm to minimize risk of infection.

Both she and Ms. Rodes were evaluated as a team by taking two tests for registration through Pet Partners®, formerly the Delta Society, a non-profit organization dedicated to the investigation of the animal-human bond. The Pet Partners® Skills Test determined Heidi's level of obedience in particular situations. The Pet Partners® Aptitude Test mimicked a visit to a facility. All of the Four-Footed Ministerial teams working here at Maryville are registered Pet Partners®. Overall, it appeared that the 2004 research confirmed the validity of using dogs in ministry. However, this study indicated that more research was needed.

SLIDE 7

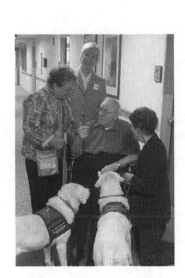

FOUR-FOOTED MINISTERS PASTORAL-CARE PROGRAM

What We Did in the Maryville Study (2011)

1. Population – 9 Pre-Screened Residents.

2. Visits – once per week beginning in September 2010; study complete May 2011. Program continues beyond study.

3. Goal – offer pastoral and spiritual care for residents, their families, and staff.

4. Time for Visits: Thursday, between 10 a.m. and 12 noon.

5. Have both individual and group interactions with Four-Footed Ministers.

Resident with Barbara Miller, Sister Josephine Pelster, SSMO, and Jerilyn. The two Four-Footed Ministers are Caterina on the left and Alya on the right.
Photo by Tom Miller, 2011

SCRIPT: This brings us the study that defined the Maryville Four-Footed Ministers Pastoral-Care Program.

This slide provides the particulars on the study conducted from September 2010 to May 2011. At its conclusion, a survey was taken to determine the value of the program. As the residents in the study overwhelmingly confirmed its importance, it has become a continuing part of the spiritual/pastoral-care program here at Maryville.

Pet Partners® dogs visit on Thursday from 10 a.m. to noon. The dogs have a limit of two-hour-per-day shifts, so the FFM teams will make every effort to visit as many individuals as they can. Part of the visitation schedule will be a dog-ministry prayer-group gathering that meets at 11 a.m. on visitation days.

The goal for this program is to offer spiritual care and comfort to residents, their families, and staff. Because of safety issues, if senior staff determines visitation is NOT appropriate for a resident, that person will not be included in the visitation schedule.

To assist our volunteer teams, the Four-Footed Ministers Pastoral-Care program coordinator or chaplain will be present to accompany the Pet Partners®-registered teams as they visit.

SLIDE 8

FOUR-FOOTED MINISTERS PASTORAL-CARE PROGRAM
THE AMERICAN CULTURE VIEW OF PETS

Dogs are part of the family.

Many residents had dogs and cannot have them now.

Thank you for understanding the residents' need to interact with the Four-Footed Ministers.

SCRIPT: This slide points out that the American culture treats animals much differently than other cultures. It is important for all to understand that the patients/residents often have had to leave their pet when they came to Maryville and many of them experience grief at losing their beloved animal. The volunteers in the Four-Footed Ministers Pastoral-Care Program want to assist these residents in dealing with this loss by providing them with the opportunity to interact with *their* dog on a consistent basis.

The members of the spiritual/pastoral-care team thank you for attempting to understand this important connection that the Four-Footed Minister is trying to keep alive through his or her presence and the availability of the dog for being touched and caressed.

SLIDE 9**

FOUR-FOOTED MINISTERS PASTORAL-CARE PROGRAM
A ONE-ON-ONE PASTORAL VISIT

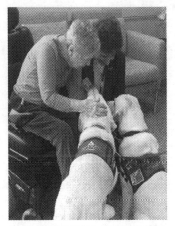

Resident with Caterina, Alya and Jerilyn

Visitation by a
Four-Footed Ministerial Team

The Four-Footed Ministerial team will normally be accompanied by the FFMPC program coordinator. The volunteer's job is to engage the resident to interact with the dog.
After a short while, the program coordinator will ask questions and listen to the resident's concerns and needs. If appropriate, a prayer will be offered. As they leave the program coordinator will offer a blessing if appropriate.

**Note that for "volunteer"/spiritual-care provider training, there are two additional slides, Slides 9 A and 9 B that explain the specifics for each volunteer role.

SLIDE 10

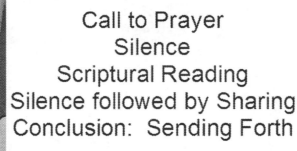

FOUR-FOOTED MINISTERS PASTORAL-CARE PROGRAM

DOG-MINISTRY PRAYER-GROUP GATHERING: WHAT IT LOOKS LIKE

Call to Prayer
Silence
Scriptural Reading
Silence followed by Sharing
Conclusion: Sending Forth

Jerilyn with resident petting Caterina.
Photo by Tom Miller, 2010.

SCRIPT: As was mentioned, there will be a dog-ministry prayer-group gathering available for residents and on the screen is an outline of how that will work.

It will begin with a call to prayer then a time of silence for reflection and centering. A selection taken from scripture or a story from another religious source concerning an animal will be read. For example, there is a story from the Catholic tradition, the Book of Tobit, where the author specifically mentions a dog who accompanies the main characters on their adventures (Tobit 6: 2 ff and 11: 1-4). There will then follow a time for reflection to consider a question based on a theme such as loyalty. Participants will be invited to share pet stories and reflect further on how their own pet stories enhance their relationship to God. At the dismissal, residents will be encouraged to take their insights into their daily dealings with others.

SLIDE 11

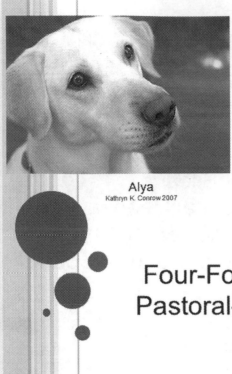

Alya
Kathryn K. Conrow 2007

Thank You for Your Attention!

The Four-Footed Ministerial teams

Wish You

Blessings on your life journey!

Four-Footed Ministers
Pastoral-Care Program

Time for questions

Dismiss

The PowerPoint presentation is based on the staff-training one. The general format is the same for "volunteer" or spiritual/pastoral-care provider with the insertion of one role-specific slide to be inserted after Slide 9:

SLIDE 9 A spiritual-care provider

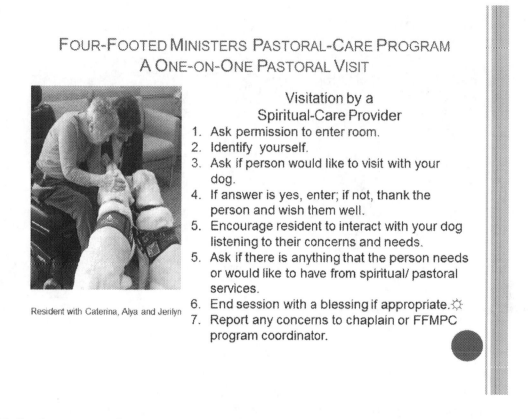

FOUR-FOOTED MINISTERS PASTORAL-CARE PROGRAM
A ONE-ON-ONE PASTORAL VISIT

Visitation by a
Spiritual-Care Provider
1. Ask permission to enter room.
2. Identify yourself.
3. Ask if person would like to visit with your dog.
4. If answer is yes, enter; if not, thank the person and wish them well.
5. Encourage resident to interact with your dog listening to their concerns and needs.
5. Ask if there is anything that the person needs or would like to have from spiritual/ pastoral services.
6. End session with a blessing if appropriate.☼
7. Report any concerns to chaplain or FFMPC program coordinator.

Resident with Caterina, Alya and Jerilyn

SCRIPT: On the screen, there are a series of steps that outline a normal interaction between a spiritual/pastoral-care provider and a Maryville resident. [READ THE STEPS]

SLIDE 9 B—Volunteer

FOUR-FOOTED MINISTERS PASTORAL-CARE PROGRAM
A ONE-ON-ONE PASTORAL VISIT

Resident with Caterina, Alya and Jerilyn

Visitation by a Volunteer

1. The chaplain or FFMPC program coordinator will ask permission to enter room and will identify herself and her volunteer.
2. If answer is yes, the team will enter; if not, she will thank the person and wish them well.
3. The chaplain or FFMPC program coordinator *will take the lead in all interchanges,* encouraging the resident to interact with the volunteer's dog listening to their concerns and needs. The volunteer present to act as the advocate for the dog in this instance.
4. The chaplain or FFMPC program coordinator will end the session offering a blessing if appropriate.☼

SCRIPT: On the screen, there are a series of steps that outline how a "volunteer" Four-Footed Ministerial team visits with the FFMPC program coordinator or chaplain. The volunteer in this instance is an advocate for the dog, taking direction from the FFMPC program coordinator or chaplain. This person functions in the same role as a volunteer would in animal-assisted therapy, but the goal is spiritual rather than physical or psychologically therapeutic. [READ THE STEPS]

INDEX